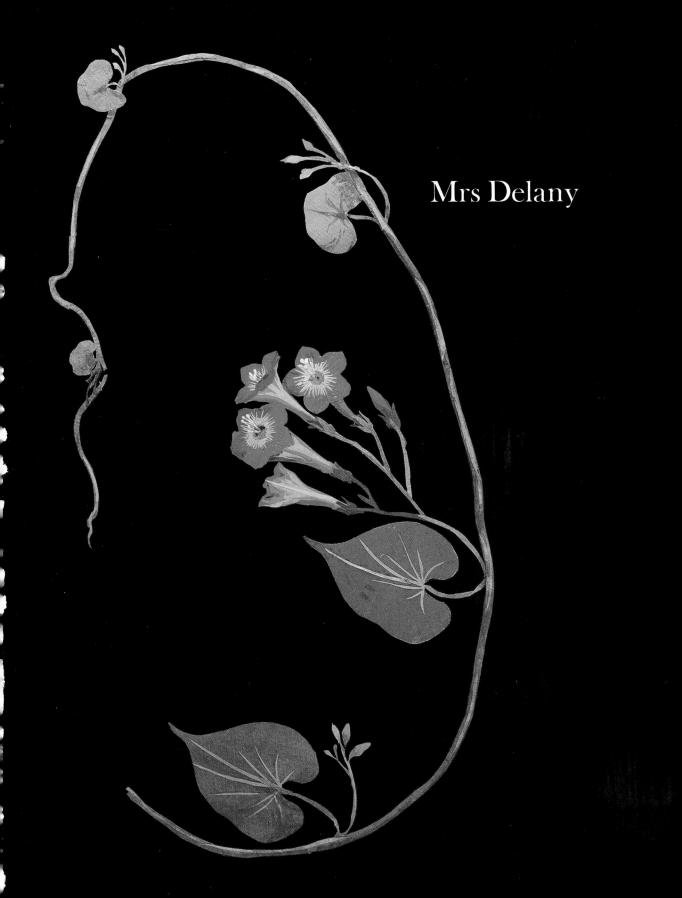

Mrs Delany

Mrs Delany

her life and her flowers

Ruth Hayden

NEW AMSTERDAM
New York

To Freddy,
remembered with love,
and to
Katie and Mark
and their families

© 1980 Ruth Hayden

Reprinted in 1986

New edition 1992

First published in the United
States of America in 1993 by
New Amsterdam Books,
NY, 10016, by arrangement with
British Museum Press, London.

Illustration on p. 1: 'Scarlet-flower'd Ipomea, Ipomea Coccinea'
[*Quamoclit coccinea*]
Frontispiece: *Mrs Delany*, by Opie

**Library of Congress Cataloguing in Publication Data
is available.**

ISBN 1–56131–061–1

Designed by Humphrey Stone
Cover designed by Slatter-Anderson
Set in Monophoto Baskerville
and printed in Great Britain by The Bath Press Ltd., Bath, Avon

Contents

Acknowledgements

The black and white photographs were obtained from: The Trustees of the British Museum pp. 33, 44, 53, 55, 123, 128; British Museum (Natural History) p. 114; British Museum Press pp. 17, 26, 67, 75, 82, 118, 124, 130, 131, 133, 136 (lower), 139, 140, 141, 142, 145, 152, 156, 162, 163, 168 (top), 172 (courtesy of the Trustees of the British Museum); Christie's Fine Art p. 89; Courtauld Institute pp. 23 (courtesy of Lord Bath), 34 (courtesy of the Trustees of the British Museum), 39, 66, 88, 92 (upper right); Ruth Hayden pp. 16, 18, 21, 27, 28 (upper), 36, 37, 38, 48, 52, 56, 61, 73, 74, 84, 90, 91, 93, 94, 96, 100, 101, 102, 103, 105, 110, 111, 112, 113, 136 (upper), 166; Longleat Collection pp. 50, 65, 81, 115, 165; Paul Mellon Centre for Studies in British Art p. 117 (courtesy of Viscount Lambton); Museum of London p. 121; National Gallery of Ireland pp. 63, 68, 86, 87, 171; National Portrait Gallery pp. 46 (courtesy of L. G. Stopford-Sackville, Esq.), 169; National Trust pp. 28, 62; Royal Collection pp. 104, 157 (copyright reserved); Courtesy of the Board of Trustees of the V & A pp. 92, 134; The Walker Art Gallery p. 164; Windsor Castle, Royal Library, © 1992 Her Majesty The Queen p. 168 (bottom).

The colour photograph on the frontispiece is reproduced by courtesy of the Trustees of the National Portrait Gallery; those on pages 60, 97 and 98 are the property of Ruth Hayden. All others are the property of British Museum Press (courtesy of The Trustees of the British Museum).

The author and publishers are grateful to all copyright holders for permission to reproduce the photographs.

Preface

As children my sisters and I were instructed by our father, a clergyman, that if the house should catch fire there were two items which should be rescued first, his sermons and the Delany. The latter was a reference to a magnificent panel of embroidery which hung in our house, part of the court dress of our ancestress Mrs Delany, which she had designed and embroidered herself. Though conscious that Mrs Delany was a fine and gifted woman of the eighteenth century, it was not until middle-age that I began to be interested in her life, encouraged by the chance to study six 'dusty old books' left in my house by a relative. The books contained Mrs Delany's letters to her sister Anne, and to her niece Mary, together with those from her friends. The letters, which had been edited by Mrs Delany's great-great-niece Lady Llanover in the mid-nineteenth century, have a style and sincerity of writing which makes them, for me, compulsive reading: their variations in spelling, which provide amusing interest, have been preserved in this book.

In addition to constituting an autobiography of Mrs Delany's life, the letters give a running commentary on events of the period and on the social life within the circle of her family and friends. As one who moved amongst those who set the fashion and who was a perceptive observer of the scene, her comments on clothes and customs as she travelled through England and Ireland are entertaining. With a remarkable degree of detail she recorded the style and design of the houses which she visited, sometimes adding historical interest by making sketches in her note book of their parks.

The study of the original letters in the Newport Reference Library, Gwent, since the publication of the first edition of *Mrs Delany* has allowed greater insights into Mrs Delany's life; it has also revealed the Victorian views of Lady Llanover as to what she felt was proper to be printed in 1861 and 1862. Although many extracts of gossip were chosen by Lady Llanover in her editing in the nineteenth century this new edition includes 'Tittle Tattle of the Tea Table', hitherto unpublished, to show Mrs Delany's human nature. More poignant are the letters she chose to omit written by Mrs Delany's married niece in 1784, showing the dread of many pregnancies, and the prolonged illnesses that nowadays would soon be despatched by modern medicine and warmer houses.

I am conscious that without the help of many kind people I could never have undertaken such an enjoyable task. Particularly I am indebted to Mr Paul Mellon, whose generosity has enabled so many coloured illustrations to be included. To the following I am equally grateful for their co-operation and generosity: Mrs Peter du Croz, Mrs Jo Flemming, the family of the late Mrs Richard Granville, Mrs O. A. Oakes, Mrs Wilkinson Riddle, Mrs J. S. Vaughan and Mrs M. Whytehead. To Mr Dudley Snelgrove go my special thanks for permission to study Mrs Delany's drawings and for his many kindnesses.

My thanks go also to the Countess Mountbatten of Burma, Sir Richard Hamilton Bt, the late Revd M. Bland, and to Miss Caroline Whiteford of the Natural History Museum. For botanical research I am indebted to Miss Sylvia FitzGerald, Chief Librarian and Archivist at the Royal Botanic Gardens, Kew, to Mr David McClintock and the late Miss Alice M. Coats, and to Miss Eleanor Booker for checking botanical lists.

At Windsor Castle I have been assisted by Mr Oliver Everett, Librarian and the Hon. Mrs Jane Roberts, Curator of the Print Room; at Newport Reference Library, Gwent by Mrs S. Pugh and her staff; and by the keeper of the Print Room at the National Gallery, Dublin.

For the success of the 'Delany' exhibition in the Pierpont Morgan Library, New York in 1986, I am indebted to Professor C. Ryskamp, Mrs Sally Aall, and Miss Sybil Connolly; for the equally appreciated exhibition two years later in Bath, to Miss Barley Roscoe, Curator at the Holburne Museum, and her staff; to Mr Bill Drummond and Mr Jacob Simon, Curator of Eighteenth-Century Portraits at the National Portrait Gallery, and to Mr P. Palmer of Dorney Court for information on drawings and portraits.

My gratitude goes to the late Mr E. Malins and the late Mr Edward St Maur; Mrs Stella M. Newton and Dr Eileen Ribeiro of the Courtauld Institute.

To my many hosts and hostesses in both north and south Ireland whose warmth of hospitality I have been fortunate to enjoy, particular mention must be given to Mr and Mrs Gordon Brickenden of Cratloe Woods whose collection of botanical collages I examined, and to Mr Joe Mahon of Irvinestown, County Fermanagh for the erection of a plaque to Dr Delany in Mahon's Hotel.

I am grateful too to Miss Celia Clear of British Museum Press for her generous guidance through what was to me new territory, and also to her colleague Miss Jenny Chattington for her extensive research on my behalf. I am especially grateful to Miss Sarah Derry whose youthful vision has brought refreshing insight to this new edition; to the late Mr Paul Hulton for his Introduction, and to Miss Hilary Williams and the staff of the Department of Prints and Drawings at the British Museum for making the study of the 'paper mosaicks' such a continued pleasure.

To my gallant husband Freddy, who encouraged and supported me throughout, and undertook many domestic duties to give me time to write, I shall forever be grateful. To Katie and Mark who have had to listen to continued chatter from me about Mrs Delany, as I have enjoyed every moment of research into a life that has been truly inspiring; to them and many others I am indebted.

RUTH HAYDEN

1992

9

Introduction

By the 1780s – she was as old as the century – Mrs Delany had
become something of a legend. She embodied for her contemporaries, particularly the younger set, virtues which were
admired as characteristic of the passing age of enlightenment:
propriety, style and wit. She was also widely loved for her goodness
of heart, a virtue perhaps less commonly found in combination with
the others. The much younger Fanny Burney wrote of her as one of
the 'Old Wits' in whom taste and discrimination excelled. An
equally devoted admirer, Hannah More, enjoyed not only her
'excellent mind' but also found in her a 'living library of
knowledge', for she had known many of the greatest men and
women of her time and had personal experience of many of its
historical events. The range of her interests and social contacts was
very wide. She was the friend of Handel, corresponded wittily with
Swift, was the niece of Lord Lansdowne, poet and patron of Pope,
knew Burke, was wooed by John Wesley, entertained and was
entertained by Garrick, and saw much of Lord Chesterfield in
Ireland. Her close friendship with the Duchess of Portland brought
her in contact with some of the greatest botanists, horticulturalists
and botanical artists of the time – Sir Joseph Banks, Solander,
Lightfoot, Fothergill, Philip Miller and Ehret among others. Her
contacts with the world of art were as strong as with that of music.
She knew Hogarth and may have had drawing lessons from him as
she had lessons in painting from Goupy. Sir Joshua Reynolds
praised her flower collages, or 'paper-mosaicks', Opie and Barber
painted her portrait and Sir Thomas Lawrence drew her in old age.
Horace Walpole in his *Anecdotes of Painting* first published her 'new
form of art'. King George III and Queen Charlotte, who also became
deeply interested in her 'mosaicks', were on terms of intimate

friendship with her and brought her comfort and happiness in her last years.

Her personality is vividly reflected in her much undervalued letters which with an autobiographical sketch were published by Lady Llanover in 1861–2. All her attributes are there – gaiety, wit, strong views, humanity and a deep and genuine piety. Yet the correspondence and her 'Essay on Propriety', written for her great-niece Georgina aged six in 1777, do not tell us the whole story. She was highly principled enough occasionally to defy convention, though she was by nature and upbringing intensely conservative. For example she was one of the group of women who besieged the House of Lords in 1739 and gained admittance against all the regulations and orders of the Chancellor – an early dent in the armour of male supremacy. Of far greater significance was her decision, against the wishes of her aristocratic family and particularly her brother's very strong opposition, to marry Dr Patrick Delany, an Irish clergyman of humble origin and comparatively modest means. This marriage unlocked strong creative elements in her. Their mutual pleasure in their garden at Delville near Dublin in particular, his encouragement of her gardening, painting, shell-work and needlework resulted in a surge of activity in a variety of media in all of which the basic theme was the flower, whether in stocking the Delville garden, painting garden landscapes, decorating interiors with shells, or working embroideries. The gathering and observation of wild flowers was vital to this creative work and Mrs Delany never neglected it. Though these activities are described in detail in her letters, the results have either disappeared or remained hidden from view ever since, so that she has won little credit for the outstanding artistry of her needlework and shell-work. This intensely happy and creative marriage prepared the way for a new artistic venture later in life.

After Dr Delany's death in 1768 her close friendship with the Duchess of Portland gave her creative powers a new stimulus. Her inborn love of nature, eye for detail, and intelligent curiosity all fed on the fine garden at Bulstrode and on the scientific information on plants provided by many of the famous men who were invited there. In addition, the outstandingly beautiful flower drawings which Ehret made at Bulstrode must have been an inspiration to Mrs Delany, whose own artistic gifts were so largely centred on flowers. Her *Flora Delanica*, as she frivolously called her collection of 'paper-mosaicks', may have begun as she says by chance but the elements which came together to create this new work had been in evidence for a long time: the ability to use scissors to cut a line as others would draw it; and a sharp eye for the details and the character of a plant; a highly developed sense of colour; and fingers which, as in her needlework, could accomplish small precise movements with absolute control. Add to these her growing understanding of the structure of plants, classified now according to the sexual system of Linnaeus, and it is surprising that she started her 'mosaicks' so late in life.

What exactly did this work amount to, which Sir Joseph Banks and so many others encouraged her to carry through until almost a thousand plants were represented and only failing sight forced her to give up as an old lady of eighty-two? For these 'mosaicks' are collages built up of often very small, separately cut pieces of coloured paper representing not only conspicuous details but also contrasting colours or shades of the same colour so that every effect of light is caught. Take for example the Damask Rose (p. 109). The stems of the spray do not consist of one shaped strip of paper but are made up of a number of variously shaded smaller strips superimposed to indicate the play of light. The fine spines each belong to one narrow strip but are separately cut out. The indented edges of the leaves are most convincingly cut and the imposed ribs give a strong three-dimensional effect. The flower buds, at various stages of opening, are beautifully worked and the contrasting shades of pink entirely convincing. The crowning glory is of course the open flower built up of numerous pieces of paper, varying from the deepest rose to the palest pink and cut in almost rococo forms, giving a wonderfully rich texture, and the stamens above the yellow-green eye, which shows signs of painting, are made up of tiny rectangular pieces of pale yellow paper. A magnifying glass reveals the complexity of the plant's construction, though it blurs the intended image. Here, in Horace Walpole's words, are 'precision and truth unparalleled'. The precision was botanical and was usually sufficient for Banks to identify each plant. The truth was art of a new kind.

It is a curious fact that Mrs Delany's flower collages are not more widely known and valued. Perhaps it is because they have never come into general circulation like the work of other great botanical artists. Or is it because they were the work of a woman which in a masculine world were thought of as charming and extraordinary but not taken very seriously? Even today, though she has her devoted admirers, some think of her 'paper-mosaicks' as the genteel work of an old lady to be compared, say, with samplers. Perhaps the details of her art given in the following pages and the reproductions in this book will help to correct such a serious misconception and to establish her in the minds of the interested public as a gifted and highly original artist.

PAUL HULTON
Deputy keeper, Prints and Drawings
British Museum

1 *Mary Granville*

In the summer of 1700, in the little Wiltshire village of Coulston, Mary Granville gave birth to her second child, a daughter, also named Mary. The baby was born into a family with a tradition of loyalty and service to the Crown. Her father, Colonel Bernard Granville, was at one time Lieutenant Governor of Hull, and had been Member of Parliament for Fowey in Cornwall. His grandfather was Sir Bevil, killed while fighting for Charles I in the Civil War, and Sir Bevil's grandfather was the famous Sir Richard Grenville, who died after a heroic encounter between his ship *Revenge* and the Spanish fleet in the reign of Queen Elizabeth I.

When Mary was still very young her parents moved to London, and at the age of six she was sent to a school for twenty pupils run by Mademoiselle Puelle, a French refugee. Mary's skill at cutting paper was noticed early at school and she was only eight when a fellow pupil, Lady Jane Douglas, so admired the little birds and flowers cut by Mary that she took some home to frame.

London was then an unhealthy place in which to live and in the hope that his wife's health, which had begun to deteriorate, would benefit, Colonel Granville moved his family a few miles away to the village of Little Chelsea, a fashionable retreat for the well-to-do. Mary, however, was sent to live in Whitehall with her father's sister, Lady Stanley, who had been a Maid of Honour to Queen Mary; it was intended that Mary should be groomed for a similar position. Lady Stanley's husband, Sir John, was secretary to the Lord Chamberlain, and so Mary grew up close to the life of the Court. At first she protested vehemently at being removed from the school, where she had been happy among her friends. Lady Stanley ran a serious household and insisted upon discipline, which frequently curbed Mary's high spirits, but her aunt and uncle were kind to her

FAR LEFT Sir Bernard Granville (b. 1596), killed in the Battle of Lansdown, 1643.

LEFT Colonel Bernard Granville, Mary's grandfather.

and she acknowledged their wisdom when she wrote many years later: 'The train of mortification that I have met with since, convince me it was happy for me to have been early inured to disappointments and vexations.'

Her aunt and uncle watched carefully over her education, which included English, French, history, music, needlework and dancing; these last three especially were considered essential qualifications for any gentlewoman. To encourage Mary with her music she was given her own harpsichord, and one day she had the pleasure of hearing it played by Handel. She was immediately struck by the beauty of his playing and the moment he left the house she sat down to imitate it as best she could. Her uncle, teasing her, asked if she thought she would ever play as well as Handel: 'If I did not think I should, I would burn my instrument!' she replied. This was her first meeting with the great composer whose friendship later she was to value.

The lighter side of life was provided by her second cousins, the children of Lord and Lady Hyde, who also lived in Whitehall. Catherine Hyde was the same age as Mary and, sharing her high spirits, became a special friend. In adult life Mary was to watch with considerable interest Catherine's progress as the witty and eccentric Duchess of Queensbury.

The death of Queen Anne in 1714 brought a sudden reversal in the fortunes of Mary's family and dealt a fatal blow to Mary's hopes

'Catherine Hyde, the Duchess of Queensbury'. Oil painting by Mrs Delany.

of a position at Court as Maid of Honour. Since the Queen had no direct heir, the Jacobite party, which the Granvilles supported, had hoped to restore the exiled Stuarts to the throne. The Whig party, however, were now in power, and they managed to carry through the succession of George, Elector of Hanover, although this did not put an end to the Jacobites' manoeuvrings. Early in 1715 Colonel Granville's brother George, Lord Lansdowne, was arrested for inciting a rebellion in the West Country. Colonel Granville decided to leave London with his wife and children and made plans for their secret departure. Unfortunately, the man from whom he hired the carriages suspected that the family were planning to flee the country and alerted the office of the Secretary of State in the hope of reward; one night the family were woken by armed soldiers in the house and arrested. Fortunately for Mary and her younger sister Anne, Lady Stanley heard what was afoot and arrived in time to persuade the soldiers to give the girls into her care. They did not, therefore, share

The reception of George I at St James's Palace, 1714.

their father's detention, which, in any case, was only of short duration, as he had too little money and political influence to be of any danger to the new government.

In November 1715 the Granville family at last set out for the manor at Buckland in Gloucestershire, made available to them by relatives. The state of the roads in England at this time was deplorable, and journeys could be long and difficult, especially in winter; it took the Granvilles five days to travel the hundred miles from London to Buckland. It was a dreary journey, and for Mary particularly sad, for she was leaving behind all that seemed most enjoyable in life. At fifteen, she had begun to enter the fashionable social world. She had been to her first play and her first opera, *Hydaspes*, in which the great Italian Nicolini had sung. She had seen and admired the exquisite clothes worn by her uncle and aunt and their friends attending Court functions, and had looked forward to the day when she, as a Maid of Honour, would share in all this splendour. Instead she was on her way to a small remote village to live in very reduced circumstances. As the youngest of three brothers, Bernard Granville had not been able to count on a large family fortune, but had depended on his offices at Court, which, of course, he had now lost. His small personal fortune was to be augmented by an allowance from his brother George.

RIGHT 'Campanula Latifolia, Giant Throatwort', one of eleven campanulas in the collection.

Buckland Manor House, from an old print.

18

Mary Westcombe, Mrs
Granville, Mary's mother.

LEFT 'Rubus odoratus, sweet flow^g
Rasberry' (in her index Mrs
Delany called this 'American
Raspberry').

The Granvilles' isolation in their new home was made worse by
the severe winter weather when they first arrived, which made any
social life impossible. Mary's father, of whom she was very fond,
exerted himself to make life pleasant for them all, but her mother
found it more difficult to adapt. Mary, too, missed London and
found little to amuse her in the new routine. She practised on her
harpsichord before the family breakfast at nine o'clock, which was
followed by lessons; after this she and her sister settled to their
needlework while their father read to them. On wet days, when she
was confined to the house, Mary occupied herself by cutting paper
designs, which she stuck on the walls of her bedroom. In the
evenings she made up a four of whist with the Rector of the parish.
After a few months Mary began to find that life at Buckland had
some compensations. She became friends with Sarah Kirkham, the

21

daughter of a local clergyman, whose high spirits attracted Mary, and their friendship grew into a life-long family connection.

With the coming of spring Mary was first aroused to the beauties of nature, for her London childhood had left her ignorant of the delights of the countryside. True she had gathered nosegays at the Toll Bridge in Knightsbridge but dust churned up by coaches and carts and the stench of inadequate drains had pervaded the air. It was different at Buckland where the house faced the lovely Vale of Evesham. 'Nothing could be more fragrant and rural;' she wrote, 'the sheep and cows came bleating and lowing to the pales of the garden . . . a little clear brook run winding through a copse of young elms (the resort of many warbling birds) and fell with a cascade into the garden, completing the concert. In the midst of that copse was an arbour with a bench, which I often visited, and I think it was impossible not to be pleased with so many natural beauties and delights as I there beheld and enjoyed around me.'

In the spring of 1716 the Granvilles made a new friend. One Sunday the Rector introduced to them a handsome young man, who was immediately invited to 'beef and pudding' the next day. Robert Twyford, aged twenty-two, was one of twenty brothers and sisters and came from near Bath. The Granvilles found him a pleasant companion and he eventually stayed with them many months, falling deeply in love with Mary. But his hopes came to naught because neither of the families was able to provide money for them to marry; Mary was thankful when he left because she was embarrassed by his persistent attentions.

There was considerable delight in the family when, in September 1717, Mary received an invitation from her uncle, Lord Lansdowne, to visit him and his wife at their country seat, Longleat in Wiltshire. Lord Lansdowne had recently been released after two years' detention in the Tower of London. He was an amateur playwright and poet, but his main interests were now political. Under Queen Anne he had held several high offices, including Treasurer of the Household, and Secretary at War. Now, after his release, he intended to settle in the West Country and extend his political influence. His wife was Mary Villiers (known in the family as Laura), widow of Thomas Thynne, and her young son, also Thomas, was heir to Longleat and its estates. Lady Lansdowne was young and beautiful, but vain and superficial, and both she and her husband were extravagant.

Mary's visit began happily enough, for she was received with

Longleat from the south, by Jan Sieberechts. It was painted in 1695 and, although formal gardens were added later (see p. 50), the house would have changed little when Mary arrived in 1717.

kindness by her uncle and aunt and was once again able to enjoy the gaiety of the social life which she had tasted briefly before. But gradually life became less comfortable. Mary, who shared her uncle's literary tastes and enjoyed many hours with him reading, incurred the jealousy of Lady Lansdowne, and she became aware also of a serious quarrel between her uncle and father. Worse was in store.

One wet day a friend of Lord Lansdowne, Alexander Pendarves, arrived in the middle of dinner. Mary was much amused by his bedraggled appearance, 'his dirty boots, his large unwieldy person and his crimson countenance'. Her laughter turned to dismay when, as the days passed and Mr Pendarves stayed on at Longleat, it became obvious that she was the reason for his delay. She did all she could to discourage his attentions but found to her alarm that her uncle and aunt had no sympathy for her plight; indeed, they welcomed the prospect of a family connection with the owner of a large West Country estate. Alexander Pendarves was Member of Parliament for Launceston and Lord Lansdowne hoped to be able to increase his political influence through him by this alliance.

After two months of wretched suspense the blow fell and Mary was summoned to her uncle:

... he took me by the hand, and after a very pathetic speech of his love and care of me, and of my father's unhappy circumstances, my own want of fortune, and the little prospect I had of being happy if I disobliged those friends that were desirous of serving me, he told me of Gromio's passion for me, and his offer of settling his whole estate on me; he then, with great art and eloquence, told me all his good qualities and vast merit, and how despicable I should be if I could refuse him because he was not young and handsome ...

Mary's feelings can well be imagined; to be married at seventeen to a man of nearly sixty, whose appearance and behaviour she found repulsive, seemed an intolerable fate. But no amount of tears or pleading moved her uncle and aunt from their set purpose: '... no one considered the sentiments of my heart; to be settled in the world, and ease my friends of an expense and care, they urged that it was my duty to submit, and that I ought to sacrifice everything to that one point.'

George Granville, Lord Lansdowne (1667–1735). Detail of oil painting by Kneller.

Mary knew that her parents would never force her to the marriage, but she knew also that they were financially dependent on Lord Lansdowne and she was afraid they would suffer if she refused. So with the greatest reluctance she acquiesced to the match, hid her distress from her parents and submitted to the awkward courtship of a man forty years her senior. It seems amazing that her fond parents were willing to accept such a husband for their daughter, but in their own straitened circumstances they were doubtless relieved that she was marrying well and were not inclined to look for disadvantages.

In the chapel at Longleat on 17 February, 1718 Mary Granville married Alexander Pendarves. Her misery was plain for all to see but her parents believed it was the thought of leaving her relatives that was the cause and not any dislike of her bridegroom. Mary wrote:

I was married with *great pomp*. Never was woe drest out in gayer colours, and when I was led to the altar, I wished from my soul I had been led, as Iphigenia was, to be sacrificed.

2 *A Marriage of Convenience*

The Pendarves remained at Longleat for two months after the wedding, waiting for the winter weather to improve before travelling to Cornwall. During this time Alexander tried to show tenderness to Mary in his clumsy way, and she did her best to reciprocate but 'had he known how much it cost me, he must have thought himself obliged by my behaviour'.

With the improved travelling conditions in April they set out for Roscrow Castle accompanied by Mary's elder brother Bernard. They stayed with friends of Alexander's along the route, though Mary would have preferred the anonymity of an inn or to have 'hidden in a cave'; the journey was slow and uncomfortable, the coach overturned several times, the roads became progressively worse, but at last after two weeks they arrived at the house.

The sight of her new home was a great shock to Mary. A huge gate in the granite wall which surrounded it opened to reveal a prison-like, desolate house, which had not been inhabited for thirty years. Alexander led her into the gloomy hall, with its smell of stale air and decaying wood; in the parlour she found the floor was rotten and the ceiling falling in. She could not even see out of the windows for the sills came only to the top of her head; overwhelmed with misery she threw herself sobbing into a chair.

But Roscrow had its compensations. Mary loved the panoramic view from the attic windows, for the house stood on a hill overlooking Penryn and Flushing, their gardens and orchards clinging prettily to the cliff edge; beyond was Falmouth, its harbour filled with shipping. Whenever she could, Mary escaped from the house to ride with Bernard over this new country.

After a month Alexander proposed that they should visit his niece Mary, wife of Francis Bassett of Tehidy, whom he had intended to

The beautiful countryside around Roscrow was a consolation for Mary during her unhappy marriage. This old print shows a view from Penryn towards Flushing.

make his heir. Mr Bassett, subdued over the years by his dull wife, found his spirits returning with the charming Mary Pendarves as his guest, who, enjoying his jokes, laughed for the first time since arriving in Cornwall. With innocent enjoyment Mary accompanied Bernard and Mr Bassett on a boat trip to the Gull Rocks, fished for mackerel, and rode along the shore looking for shells 'which I took a great delight in'. From this initial interest later developed her wonderful skill in shell-work, for she was to decorate grottoes, ceilings, mantelpieces and chandeliers of her own design.

These delightful outings were sadly cut short by Alexander's jealousy; one day he burst into tears and warned Mary against Mr Bassett, 'a cunning treacherous man, he has been the ruin of one woman already, who was the wife to his bosom friend'. This was yet another problem for Mary to contend with: as the young bride of a gout-ridden, elderly husband she was to find herself considered fair game for wayward males both in the country and in London.

There was the alarming affair with Mr Newman, a guest at Roscrow, whom the Pendarves noticed was becoming increasingly

26

morose. Alone with Mary he suddenly seized her hands and, looking wildly into her face, said he wished he had never met her and that she was the reason for his unhappiness. Tearing herself away she fled into her dressing-room and locked the door behind her, terrified that Alexander might have seen them, and wondering how she could get Mr Newman removed. Fortunately that evening a servant informed Alexander of Mr Newman's request for a pistol and Alexander, still unaware of the incident with Mary, decided that his unbalanced guest must be told to go. Mr Newman left for the house of a friend, whose sister he seduced before he died, insane, a year later.

In the second year of this sad marriage Mary was confined to the house more often, nursing her husband, for Alexander's gout was frequently bad and kept him at home. He was fortunate in having a wife who enjoyed reading and working with her hands. During the long hours spent at Alexander's bedside, she developed such mastery over her needle that she came to interpret nature through embroidery with a skill and delicacy unrivalled in that century. Alexander was pleased with her attentions and became fond of her, but, try as she might, Mary could not regard him with anything but repugnance:

. . . he was excessively fat, of a brown complexion, negligent in his dress, and took a vast quantity of snuff, which gave him a dirty look: his eyes were black, small, lively and sensible; he had an honest countenance but altogether a person rather disgusting than engaging.

A section of a white, three-cornered tiffany handkerchief worked by Mary. Lady Llanover described this as the 'most wonderful of all her works.' The handkerchief was attached to the top of the bodice; the curved cut-out edge fitted around the neck.

In the third year of their marriage business affairs took Alexander to London and Mary enjoyed a visit from her family: 'O *happy year!* that made me some amends for what I had suffered.' But in 1721, finding he must stay yet another year in London, Alexander sent for Mary to join him. She spent a month at her old home in Buckland and took the opportunity to arrange the baptism of her black servant John. It was the fashion in the eighteenth century for the more wealthy members of society to employ a native servant who could be seen riding on the outside of a coach smartly dressed in the owner's livery. Thus Mary set out for London.

At the house which Alexander had taken in Rose Street, Hog Lane, Soho, Mary found her husband's ill-tempered sister installed, a silly foolish woman whose husband had run off with her money. Alexander had rejoined his old drinking friends and would return intoxicated between six and seven in the morning, needing two servants to put him to bed. He blamed a cheating steward and bad tenants for their need to economise. Poor Mary, she was losing the one asset – substantial financial security – that had been assured her by Lord and Lady Lansdowne in this wretched marriage.

After the quiet and unsophisticated social round in Cornwall Mary was delighted to see so many of her friends again. London was buzzing with activities, and she was glad to leave the house whenever she could. There were Lady Stafford's assemblies held every fortnight, at which Mary, with the Queen's blessing, chaperoned the Royal seamstress Miss Hays, whose indiscreet behaviour and appearance some months later 'in a loose robe' was the subject of much speculation, and an embarrassment for Mary. She attended her first masquerade wearing a black domino over her eyes, and enjoyed an evening picnic with Lady Harriet Harley, mother of Margaret Harley, who, as Duchess of Portland, was to become her devoted friend:

Last Wednesday I was all night upon the water with Lady Harriet Harley. We went into the barge at five in the afternoon and landed at Whitehall Stairs. We rowed up the river as far as Richmond, and were entertained all the time with very good musick in another barge. The concert was composed of three hautboys, two bassoons, flute, allemagne, and young Grenoc's trumpet . . . we ate some cold meat and fruit, and there was variety of wines . . .

All these events were reported fully in Mary's letters to her sister Anne. She took care to mention the clothes that had caught her eye and throughout her life Mary remained a keen observer of fashion.

Buckland Church, from an old print.

A postilion from Erddig Park, Flintshire, in the mid-eighteenth century.

RIGHT 'Hemerocallis fulva, Bruno's Lilly'.

OVERLEAF
LEFT 'Crinum Zeylanicum, Asphodil Lilly'. The plant was a gift from Lord Rockingham.
RIGHT 'Ornithogalum Arabicum', recorded in Mrs Delany's *Index* to her collages as 'Arabian Star of Bethlehem'. The ovary, filament and anther are shown.

Those who lived in the country, as Anne did, relied upon the letters of friends and relatives in the towns to keep them informed of the latest fashions. Occasions such as royal birthday celebrations, where those attending came arrayed in the finest fabrics with their most magnificent jewels, provided Mary with plenty of opportunity to comment:

There was a great many fine clothes on the birthday. Lady Sunderland was very fine and very genteel. Her clothes were the finest pale blue and pink, very richly flowered in a running pattern of silver frosted and tissue with a little white, a new Brussels head, and Lady Oxford's jewels.

It was usual for ladies, when preparing themselves for a special occasion, to receive visitors, both male and female, and whilst the frisseur curled their locks they chatted to the callers. 'I was at Lady Carteret's toilette, whose clothes were pretty, pale straw lutestring and flowered with silver, and new Brussels head.'

A lady entertains visitors in her boudoir, while the frisseur dresses her hair. *The Countess' Levée*, by Hogarth, 1745.

Weddings, too, were occasions of considerable interest, though in the eighteenth century the ceremony was generally attended by just a few of the relatives, and a reception for the guests was more often held the following day. When Margaret Rolle married Lord Walpole, Mary attended the reception. The bride looked 'excessively fine, in the handsomest and richest gold and white stuff that ever I saw, a fine point head, and very fine brilliant earings and cross. Mrs Rolle was in pink and silver lutestring, and Mrs Walpole in a white and gold and silver, but not so pretty as Mrs Rolle's.' Nothing was missed by Mary's eagle eye: 'Every body had favours that went, men and women: they are silver gauze six bows, and eight of gold narrow ribbon in the middle: they cost a guinea a piece; eight hundred has already been disposed of. Those the King, prince, princess, and the young princesses had, were gold ribbon embroidered; they were six guineas a piece.'

In 1723 Colonel Granville died and Mrs Granville and Anne moved nearer Gloucester. They were still far from the fashionable world and relied upon Mary to inform them of the unwritten rules

The Wedding Night, by Marcellus Laroon II. This lively scene shows the traditional custom of 'throwing the stocking'.

34

for mourning, which it was *de rigueur* for those in their class to observe. Three months after the death of their father Anne was told 'You should, if you keep strictly to the rules of mourning, wear your shammy gloves two months longer, but in the country if it is more convenient to you, you may wear black silk; you might have worn black earings and necklace these two months.' After twelve months' bereavement there was a change in clothing. 'My mama must not wear black handkerchiefs with her second year's mourning.' (The word handkerchief referred to the drapery or fichu forming the top of the bodice round the neck.)

Although London's social life and entertainments were a relief from the unhappiness of Mary's home, they brought their own complications, for the coxcombs and idle men about town were quick to take advantage of a handsome young unescorted wife. Fabrici, the odious and fawning Hanoverian minister, pestered her in London and even followed her to Windsor when Alexander took rooms there for a short time. Mary was walking in the park when she was suddenly confronted by Fabrici who kneeled before her, clutched her skirts, and poured out his love for her – all in full view of the window of her lodgings where Alexander sat nursing his leg. She had to threaten to complain to the King before Fabrici let her go. She was outraged and told him never even to bow to her again.

Another persistent admirer was Earl Clare, one of her Aunt Laura's cast-off lovers. Sitting at Alexander's bedside one day, Mary opened a letter brought by Lady Lansdowne's servant and was horrified to find it was from Earl Clare, begging her to run away with him. Mary had once had the courage to criticise her aunt for associating with 'free libertine people', and in revenge Lady Lansdowne tried frequently to draw her niece into love affairs. She was wasting her time; Mary's strong will and high principles protected her against any temptation to be unfaithful to her elderly, ailing husband.

The only one of her admirers to whom she felt at all drawn was Lord Baltimore, brother of her friend Charlotte Hyde. 'I thought him more agreeable than anybody I had ever known,' she wrote, 'and consequently more dangerous.'

Although Mary felt in the first years of her marriage that she had no-one in whom she could confide with complete trust, there gradually came a development in her relationship with Anne which surprised and comforted her. During the visit of her family to Roscrow in 1720 Mary had taken considerable delight in the company of her young sister, and as Anne grew into a thoughtful and mature young woman Mary began to cherish their relationship:

I was surprised at her understanding having never before attended to her but as to a child, and the goodness of her heart, and the delicacy of her sentiments delighted me still more. From that time I had a perfect confidence in her, told her some of my distresses, and found great consolation and relief to my mind by this opening of my heart, and from her great tenderness and friendship for me.

It also meant that Mary could show the more human side of her nature, repeating gossip that inevitably came her way in London society. This extract from a letter to Anne was omitted from Lady Llanover's Victorian edition of Mrs Delany's letters:

Pray let me know what new scandal you have heard of Lady Bristol, it is the present Tittle Tattle of the Tea Tables that she and Coll. Cotton was caught together at an unseasonable time. I suppose you hear that Mrs Young was found a Bed with Mr Norton, by her husband, Norton grumbled and begged his life, Young told him he would not attack his Person but his fortune, which is not considerable eno' for him to support such a prosecution without the kind assistance of his bedfellow who has lately had 15000 lb left her by her mother.

The end of Mary Pendarves' marriage to Alexander came suddenly in 1724. She had slept badly, wakened by horrible nightmares, and felt depressed all day. Alexander had spent the day with his usual friends and returned morose, but made a pathetic attempt to apologise to her for the disappointing life into which she had been inveigled. He told Mary how much he appreciated her having been a good wife to him and hoped he might live to reward her. He said he wished to remake his will in her favour, but seeing he was tired she persuaded him against sending the servant for pen and paper there and then. They retired to bed. Mary could not get to sleep until four o'clock and woke again at seven, when the servant opened the shuttered windows. As Mary pulled back the curtains of the big four-poster and slipped out of bed she glanced back at her husband. The sight was horrible for Alexander lay black in the face, dead. Terrified she ran screaming from the room.

Anne Granville, Mary's younger sister. From a drawing in crayons by Mary.

3   *A Widow in Society*

Mary Pendarves.

The trauma of Alexander's death affected Mary's health, but under the care of her uncle and aunt, Sir John and Lady Stanley, with whom she at first went to live, a tranquillity came into her life that she had not known for years. The will which should have made her heiress to Alexander's property had not been made, and so his estates passed to his niece. Mary had been left enough to provide an income of several hundred pounds a year, not the thousands she had been led to expect, but sufficient to enable her to take her place in society and live independently, though she could not afford the extravagance shown by so many of her contemporaries.

Mary, young and widowed, was determined to enjoy her freedom within the bounds of propriety. It was not long before she was out and about at the opera, enjoying Handel's new works with enthusiasm, attending masquerades and private assemblies in the houses of her friends, and enjoying herself at Court at the many royal birthday celebrations. She scrutinised every detail of the magnificent clothes with admiration and sometimes criticism: 'The King was in blue velvet, with diamond buttons; the hat was buttoned up with prodigeous fine diamonds . . . Princess Royal's gown looked poor, it being only faced and robed with embroidery.' There were walks with her friends in St James's Park and Marylebone Gardens to exchange the gossip of the day, gentle airings in the Stanley's coach in King's Road, and shopping requests to fulfil for her mother and sister. She made visits to her relatives in Gloucestershire and Herefordshire, and later made a journey to Ireland which was to be a turning point in her life.

Her social life was active and varied, but even at home she was never idle. Two examples of her work were a tippet (a small cape) composed entirely of macaw and canary feathers, and a set of chair

37

Mary was keen to try her skill at many different crafts. She made this delicate floral design by pressing leaves and flowers onto paper, after coating them with ink.

seats. The art of japanning and the collecting of shells both caught her imagination. She enjoyed drawing and painting lessons and became accomplished on the spinet.

Such an enthusiasm for life inevitably brought her suitors, but marriage was not what Mary wished for. She could not easily forget her own unhappy experience and as she looked at the lives of her friends and acquaintances she saw no reason to change her view. Of Charlotte Hyde's marriage Mary remarked: 'Matrimony! . . . there's a blessed scene before my eyes of the comforts of that state. – A sick husband, squalling brats, a cross mother-in-law, and a thousand unavoidable impertinences; no, no . . .'

Understandably Mary's marriage of convenience had left her with strong feelings about the position of women in the eighteenth century:

Why must women be *driven to the necessity* of marrying? a state that should always be a matter of *choice*! and if a young woman has not fortune sufficient to maintain her in the station she has been bred to, what can she do, but marry? and to avoid living either very obscurely or running into debt, she accepts of a match with no other view than that of interest. Has not *this* made matrimony an irksome prison to many, and prevented its being that happy union of hearts where mutual choice and mutual obligation make it the most perfect state of friendship?

She condemned the attitude of the late Lord Thanet, who:

. . . left but one daughter unmarried, Lady Bell Tufton . . . her fortune two thousand pounds, which her father has left her with this proviso, not to marry Lord Nassau Paulet – a hard injunction, as they have long had an inclination for one another. His estate is about two thousand a year, but my Lord Thanet, not thinking it sufficient for his daughter, forbids the banes; I have no patience with his memory, for who can judge of our happiness but ourselves, and if *one* thousand pound a year and a great deal of love will content me, better than *ten* thousand with indifference . . . I have no notion of love and a knapsack, but I cannot think riches the only thing that ought to be considered in matrimony . . .

In middle age she observed:

. . . there is one *error* which most fathers run into, and that is providing *too little* for daughters; young men have a thousand ways of improving a little fortune, by professions and employments, if they have good friends, but young gentlewomen have no way, the fortune settled on them is all they are to expect – they are incapable of making an addition.

Mary encouraged gentlewomen who had no private income to find employment in the houses of richer people, though she was well aware that the remuneration was far from enough to support them in old age. Seven years after Alexander's death she still felt bitter about the inferior position that women held in her century, and wrote to her sister:

Would it were so, that I went ravaging and slaying all odious men, and that would go near to clear all the world of that sort of animal; you know I never had a good opinion of them, and every day my *dislike strengthens*; some *few* I will except, but *very few*, they have so despicable an opinion of women, and

Mary enjoyed music and attended private concerts. This drawing by Marcellus Laroon shows a concert at Montagu House in 1735.

treat them by their words and actions so ungenerously and inhumanly. By my manner of inveighing, anybody less acquainted with me than yourself would imagine I had *very lately* received some ill usage. No! 'tis my general observation on conversing with them: the minutest indiscretion in a woman (though occasioned by themselves), never fails of being enlarged into a notorious crime; but men are to sin on without limitation or blame; a hard case!–not the restraint we are under, for *that I extremely approve of*, but the unreasonable license tolerated in the men.

Any sort of ceremony always interested Mary, and when George II was crowned in 1727 she had already lived through the reign of three sovereigns. She had a ticket to sit in the gallery of Westminster Hall where their Majesties were to dine. Many of Mary's friends were at the banquet and came over to speak to her and to offer her meat and bread, sweetmeats and wine, which were drawn up into the galleries from below by baskets at the end of a long string. Mary noted that the Queen's dress had jewels worth £240,000 on the front of the skirt, but nevertheless thought she did not make show enough for the occasion. Mary was particularly impressed by the eighteen hundred candles, which 'were all lighted in less than three minutes by an invention of Mr Heidegger's which succeeded to the admiration of all the spectators.'

The Coronation celebrations continued with the Lord Mayor's feast a few days later, for which Mary also had an invitation. In company with the Duchess of Manchester, Lady Carteret, and Lady Fanny Shirley, she drove through the crowded streets to King Street, where they left the carriage and continued to Guildhall on foot. They were met by the Lord Mayor's officers carrying blue and gold staffs; they showed their tickets and were conducted into the room where the Lady Mayoress and the Aldermen's ladies were seated:

Our names were told and everybody made a low curtsey to her ladyship, who returned it with a great deal of civility, and told us if we would follow her we should dine at her table–an honour not to be refused, and indeed it was a particular favour. We attended her, and had a very fine dinner, and all the polite men of our acquaintance waited behind our chairs and helped us to what we wanted . . . The King, &c, were at a house which they say has always been kept for that purpose, over against Bow church, to see the procession. His own coach and horses that conveyed him to the Hall, was covered with purple cloth; the eight horses (the beautifullest creatures of their kind), were cream colour, the trappings purple silk, and their manes and tails tied with purple riband; the Princesses' horses were black, dressed with white ribands. The King was in purple velvet, the Queen and Princesses in black, and very fine with jewels.

'Fumaria Fungosa, new Species climbing fumetory' [*Adlumia fungosa*]

'Dianthus caryophyllus, a variety Jersey Pink'

BELOW 'Fragaria Vesca, wood strawberry'

Mary watched the Lord Mayor greet their Majesties and saw them at dinner, and afterwards watched the ball from seats in the gallery refreshing herself with tea and coffee. The King and Queen left at midnight and Mary and her friends went just after one, 'not being able sooner to get to our coach.'

At Queen Caroline's birthday celebration Mary came to the notice of the Queen:

On Saturday the first day of March, it being Queen Caroline's birth-day, I dressed myself in all my best array, borrowed my Lady Sunderland's jewels, and made a tearing show . . . There was a vast Court, and my Lady Carteret got with some difficulty to the circle and after she had made her curtsey made me stand before her. The Queen came up to her, and thanked her for bringing me forward, and she told me she was *obliged to me* for my pretty clothes, and admired my Lady Carteret's extremely; she told the Queen they were my fancy, and that I drew the pattern. Her Majesty said she had heard I could draw very well (I can't think who could tell her *such a story*) . . .

At night there was a ball but the crush at these events was considerable, and on this occasion Mary lost her party: '. . . I might as well have attempted to swim cross the sea in a storm; and after having been buffeted about and crushed to a mummy, my Lord Sunderland espied me out, and made me take his place.'

Other events in the social round included weddings. They were often solemnised in the evening, as was the wedding of Mary's cousin Georgina Carteret. She was married to John Spencer, brother of Charles, Duke of Marlborough, at St George's in Hanover Square between eight and nine. The wedding was a small family occasion: 'After they were married they played a pool at commerce, supped at ten, went to bed between twelve and one'. Though only a few relatives were present their clothes were magnificent and were 'laid by for the royal wedding, which will be about three weeks hence, 'tis thought.' This particular royal wedding was that between Anne Princess Royal and William Prince of Orange on 14 March 1734, another occasion for great finery. This ceremony, too, was held in the evening with much pomp. At eleven o'clock the royal family supped in public in the great state ball-room. At about one o'clock the bride and groom retired, and were afterwards seen by the nobility sitting up in their bedchamber in rich undress.

It is not certain that Mary attended the ceremony, but she was at a party held soon after. The Princess wore:

The marriage of Princess Royal
to the Prince of Orange, 14
March 1733.

. . . a manteau and petticoat, white damask, with the finest embroidery of rich embossed gold and festoons of flowers intermixed in their natural colours. On one side of her head she had a green diamond of a vast size, the shape of a pear, and two pearls prodigiously large that were fastened to wires and hung loose upon her hair: on the other side small diamonds prettily disposed, her earrings, necklace, and bars to her stays all extravagantly fine, presents of the Prince of Orange to her. . . . The King was in a gold stuff which made much more show, with diamond buttons to his coat; his star and George shone most gloriously. The Queen's clothes were a green ground flowered with gold and several shades; but grave and very handsome; her head loaded with pearls and diamonds. . . . The Prince of Wales was fine as you may suppose, but I hardly ever remember men's clothes, [The Prince of Wales] dances better than anybody, and the Prince of Orange most surprisingly well considering his shape.

During the late 1730s the fashion for large designs on the petticoat of court dresses became increasingly popular, and it was probably this which influenced Mary when she designed and embroidered her own court dress. Selina, Countess of Huntingdon was the first person Mary saw in this new fashion:

. . . her petticoat was black velvet embroidered with chenille, the pattern a *large stone vase* filled with *ramping flowers* that spread almost over a breadth of the petticoat from the bottom to the top; between each vase of flowers was a pattern of gold shells, and foliage embossed and most heavily rich; the

44

gown was white satin embroidered with chenille mixt with gold ornaments, *no vases* on the *sleeves*, but *two or three on the tail*; it was a most laboured piece of finery, the pattern much properer for a stucco staircase than the apparel of a lady,–a mere shadow that tottered under every step she took under the load. . .

One can see how the fashion had caught on, for by 1741 there were more spectacular gowns to be seen at Norfolk House, then occupied by the Prince of Wales. Mary described Lady Scarborough's dress of violet-coloured satin, the petticoat embroidered with 'clumsy festoons of *nothing at all's supported by pillars* no better than posts, the gown covered with embroidery, a very unmeaning pattern, but altogether very fine'. It was the Duchess of Queensbury's clothes that impressed her most:

. . . they were white satin embroidered, the bottom of the petticoat *brown hills* covered with all sorts of weeds, and *every breadth* had an old *stump of a tree* that run up almost to the top of the petticoat, broken and ragged and worked with brown chenille, round which twined nastersians, evy, honeysuckles, periwinkles, convolvuluses and all sorts of twining flowers which spread and covered the petticoat, vines with the leaves variegated as you have seen them by the sun, all rather smaller than nature . . . the robings and facings were little green banks with all sorts of weeds, and the sleeves and the rest of the gown loose twining branches of the same sort as those on the petticoat: many of the leaves were finished with gold, and part of the stumps of the trees looked like the golding of the sun. I never saw a work so prettily fancied, and am quite angry with myself for not having the same thought, for it is infinitely handsomer than mine, and could not cost *much more*.

Since the death of her husband Mary had lived mainly with Sir John and Lady Stanley, either at their apartments in Somerset House or at their villa in Fulham. Her aunt's health was failing and Mary's high spirits were rather constrained by the sombre atmosphere of the household. It was in some ways a relief therefore when the death of Lady Stanley left her free to travel. In 1730 she shared a house at Richmond with a close friend, Mrs Donellan, and the following year they received an invitation to visit Mrs Donellan's brother and sister in Ireland. The two ladies set out for an intended visit of six months.

At Chester, where they were to embark for Ireland, Mary and Mrs Donellan had to wait for suitable weather before the *Pretty Betty* could set sail. While they were there they received an invitation to visit Eaton, the estate of Sir Richard Grosvenor. Mary's description of it reveals her up-to-date attitude to landscaping: it was laid out in

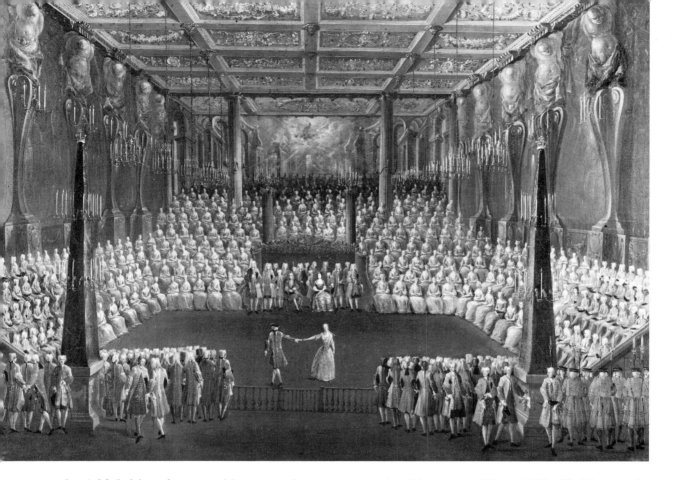

the 'old-fashioned taste with cut-work parterres and wilderness enclosed in hedges.' By 'old-fashioned taste' she was referring to the Dutch style of laying out gardens popular before the time of either Charles Bridgeman or William Kent. One of the typical features of Bridgeman's garden planning was the abandonment of walls, unless concealed as in a ha-ha. Mary may well have known Kent's work at Esher for Henry Pelham, or for Lord Burlington at Chiswick.

On arriving in Ireland they went to stay with Mrs Donellan's sister, Mrs Clayton, who was married to the Bishop of Killala. The Claytons had a house in St Stephen's Green, Dublin, and soon drew their guests into the social round centred on Dublin Castle. Mary was amused by Mrs Clayton's social pretensions. After a military review at Phoenix Park Mary wrote: 'Nobody's equippage out-looked ours except my Lord Lieutenant's, but in every respect I must say Mrs Clayton's *outshines* her neighbours'. A few weeks later at a ball everyone danced except the Duchess of Dorset and Mrs Clayton, 'who thought it beneath the dignity of a Bishop's wife to dance.'

The social life of Dublin centred around the Castle. This anonymous painting shows a state ball at Dublin Castle in the 1730s.

46

The Irish were apparently energetic dancers, and the custom there of staying with one partner all evening Mary found could be exhausting:

I had Captain Folliat, a man six foot odd inches high, black, awkward, ramping, roaring, &c. I thought he would have shook my arms off, and crushed my toes to atoms, every moment he did some blundering thing, and as often asked 'my ladyship's pardon.' . . . In the midst of his furious dancing, when he was throwing his arms about him most outrageously (just like a card scaramouch on a stick), snap went something, that we all thought had been the main bone of his leg, but it proved only a bone of his toe. Notwithstanding which (like Widdington) he fought upon his stumps, and would not spare me one dance; we began pegging it at eight, and continued our sport till one, *without ceasing*.

Needless to say she reported herself as 'almost dead' the following day. Another example of the Irish stamina for dancing was shown when Mary stayed at Plattin: 'the dancing began at seven; danced thirty-six dances with only resting once, supped at twelve, every one by their partner, at a long table which was handsomely filled with all manner of cold meat, sweetmeats, creams and jellies.' After she and some of the other ladies had sung they danced and acted plays till eight in the morning: '(very rakish indeed) went early to bed that night'.

In the spring Mary and Mrs Donellan set off for a round of visits across Ireland. This was a pastime which Mary particularly enjoyed because of her interest in the countryside, gardens and houses. Her visit to Dangan, Co. Meath, the home of the Wesleys, was particularly happy for life there was informal and fun:

We live magnificently, and at the same time without ceremony. There is a charming large hall with an organ and harpsichord, where all the company meet when they have a mind to be together, and where music, shuttlecock, draughts, and prayers, take their turn. Our hours for eating are ten, three and ten again.

Mary and Mrs Donellan continued their journey westwards, stopping at an inn at Tuam, then on to Mr Bingham's at Castlebar, and so to Newton Gore, Co. Mayo to visit Sir Arthur Gore, a jolly red-faced widower who lived with his daughter: 'his dogs and horses are *as dear* to him as his children, his laugh is hearty, though his jests are coarse.' With delightful simplicity Anne is instructed to address her letters to Mary 'at Killala, In Ireland', as the two ladies reach their destination at Dr Clayton's house.

Mary's journey across Ireland had given her an insight into life there. She was immensely struck by Irish hospitality:

The people of this country don't seem solicitous of having *good dwellings* or more furniture than is absolutely necessary – *hardly so much*, but they make it up in *eating and drinking*! I have not seen less than fourteen dishes of meat for dinner, and seven for supper . . . if we are to go to an inn they [our hosts] constantly provide us with a basket crammed with good things; no people *can be more hospitable or obliging* . . .

Nothing escaped her notice: 'The roads are much better in Ireland than England, mostly causeways, a little jumbling, but *very safe*.' But there were sad sights that met her eyes too: 'The poverty of the people as I have passed through the country has made *my heart ache*, I never saw greater appearance of *misery*, they live in great extremes, either *profusely* or *wretchedly*.'

The soft Irish air and outdoor life suited Mary admirably; she felt in the best of health, and decided to extend her visit to Ireland to eighteen months. The next three months were spent at Killala, at the Bishop's house, which stood close to the sea. This gave Mary an opportunity to pursue her interest in collecting shells, a hobby which the Bishop shared. There were excursions by boat to the islands offshore to search for them, and rides on horseback along the sandy strands, and once a hilarious ride in a cart:

. . . we were very merry . . . and we drove as jocund as ever five people were. I laughed immoderately . . . The rest of the company were conveyed home in a chaise, being too proud for carting. You must understand that we are as private in this place as heart can wish, and that we may do a hundred frolics of that kind without any other witnesses than the servants of the house.

Having collected a considerable number of shells, Mary ornamented a grotto overlooking the sea and nearby islands. She and Mrs Donellan began work at seven in the morning; the men of the party did the fetching and carrying, and probably mixed the mortar for her. This grotto in the Bishop's garden was the first of her creations in shell-work in Ireland; later her designs had greater finesse, using the technique of combining shells with stucco to decorate not only ceilings and walls in houses, but also objects such as candelabra. The success of the grotto at Killala inspired her to continue the new hobby after her return to England, where she decorated a grotto at Northend, Fulham, in her uncle's garden.

Mary's delight in the beauty of the shells was part of a general awareness of the natural world that was itself inextricably bound up with her religious views:

. . . the beauties of *shells* are as *infinite as of flowers*, and to consider how they

Shell decoration on a mantelpiece worked by Mary and Anne. The shells were sent in a barrel by Mary from Ireland.

are inhabited enlarges a field of wonder that leads one insensibly to the great Director and Author of these wonders. How surprising is it to observe the indifference, nay (more properly) *stupidity* of mankind, that seem to make no reflection as they live, are pleased with what they meet with because it has beautiful colours or an agreeable sound, there they stop, and receive but little more pleasure from them than a horse or a dog.

During the visit to Ireland Mary made two important new friendships. The first was with Dr Delany, a Protestant clergyman. She described him to her sister as a most desirable friend 'for he has all the qualities requisite for friendship, zeal, tenderness and application; I know you would like him because he is worthy.' But Dr Delany had just married a rich widow so the relationship progressed no further than friendship at that time.

At a dinner given by Dr Delany Mary met Dean Swift and was very taken with him:

Swift is a very *odd companion* (if that expression is not too familiar for so extraordinary a genius); he talks a great deal and does not require many answers; he has infinite spirits and says abundance of good things in his common way of discourse. Miss Kelly's beauty and good-humour have gained an entire conquest over him, and I come in only *a little by the by*.

But Swift took more notice of Mary than she realised. He was quick to recognise in her a woman with a perceptive and original mind, and he was intrigued. After a second meeting with him at Dr Delany's, Mary wrote: 'The Dean of St Patrick's [Swift] was there, in *very good humour*, he calls himself *"my master,"* and corrects me when I speak bad English, or do not pronounce my words distinctly.' She had indeed made her mark, and they corresponded after she returned to England. In February 1734 Swift wrote to her:

I am grown sickly, weak, lean, forgetful, peevish, spiritless – and for those very reasons expect that you, who have nothing to do but to be happy, should be entertaining me with your letters and civilities . . . *it is your fault*; why did you not come sooner into the world or let me come later? *it is your fault* for coming into Ireland at all; *it is your fault* for leaving it.

Referring to an aching eye that had afflicted Mary he wrote:

. . . the complaint you make of a disorder in one of your eyes will admit no raillery . . . I am often told that I am an ill judge of ladies' eyes, so that I shall make an ill compliment by confessing that I read in yours all the accomplishments I found in your mind and conversation, and happened to agree in my thoughts with better judges. I only wish they could never shine out of Dublin.

The correspondence continued until 1736, when Swift's failing

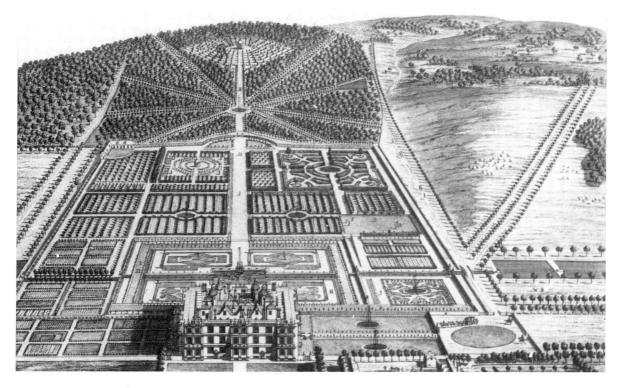

health prevented him from writing. But over thirty years later Mary was sufficiently intrigued to search his published letters: 'I have to my great mortification found six or seven letters of Mrs Pendarves there!' It was with veneration that in her old age she was to be known as 'Dean Swift's Mrs Delany'.

On her return to England in the spring of 1733, Mary made a round of visits: 'I attended Lord and Lady Weymouth down to Long Leat, and left them with as much happiness as matrimony can give.' Thomas Thynne, second Viscount Weymouth, was the son of Mary's aunt, Laura, who had shamefully neglected him. But Mary was fond of Thomas; she was ten years his senior and had looked upon him as a brother. She had considered for some time that marriage might well help to settle him away from his undoubtedly very extravagant way of life. She wrote that he was 'good-natured and affectionate but liberal without distinction, warm in his temper, could not bear contradiction'. Thomas had at one time suggested that he marry her, which she at first treated as a joke, until he kept repeating it. She firmly dismissed the suggestion, but encouraged him to marry her cousin Louisa, second daughter of Lord Carteret, who had 'a sweetness of manner (a true copy of her mind) joined to a

This print of Longleat by Knyff shows the formal gardens in the French and Dutch styles. These gardens had fallen into decay by 1757, when they were superseded by Capability Brown's landscaping.

pretty genteel person, that made her very engaging . . . her fortune was small, but she had been bred up in magnificence, and knew how to spend a large one gracefully and manage it prudently'. Mary considered Louisa eminently suitable to grace the Longleat household, and she was more than delighted when the couple were married in 1733.

From Longleat she went to Gloucester to her mother and sister. In Mary's accounts of life in the country one is immediately aware that she is writing of a different level of society. Their circle was an unsophisticated one, made up of successful traders and country squires, and the occasional officer in the militia. The contrast is made plain in her letter to Lady Throckmorton:

Gloucester affords so little variety, that I can send you no accounts from hence worthy your notice; we have assemblies once a week, such as they are, and we go because we would not be thought churlish. They are made up of an odd mixture, and if my sister and myself loved pulling people to pieces, we should find material enough, to exercise our wits upon – at least excellent food for ill nature.

But if the local company was limited in intellectual stimulation, Mary was never happier than with Anne. The sisters shared the same outlook on life. Though Anne appeared the quieter of the two, this was probably because of her comparative seclusion in the country. When they were apart, Mary poured out all her thoughts to Anne in her letters. She often referred to their friendship, that word having a far deeper meaning then than it does in the twentieth century: 'A strong and faithful friendship! that's the true zest of pleasure, the refinement of life, which mends the heart, and mitigates a thousand sorrows. A fairy spot of ground to be enjoyed with a friend is preferable to the whole world without happiness.'

Mary advised and encouraged Anne in the art of cut-paper. Of some design that Anne had cut and sent to her she wrote:

The little poppets are very well cut, but you must take more pains about the trees and shrubs, for no white paper must be left, and the leaves must be shaped and cut distinctly round the edges of the trees; most of the paper I have cut has cost me much pains as if it was white paper.

Such fineness of work was to become one of the most important aspects of her art of botanical illustration in cut paper which was to bring so many hours of happy employment to her in old age.

Anne was not physically strong, and Mary was often concerned for her sister's health. Her letters to Anne sometimes give interesting

For Mary, fineness of work was essential in cut-paper work. Her skill is shown in this picture of deer in Bulstrode Park, measuring just 4 inches in diameter.

glimpses of popular eighteenth-century cures. After Anne had chicken-pox she was advised by Mary to take a draught of rotten-apple water night and morning, 'the rottenest apples that can be had, put into a cold still, and so distilled, without anything besides'. She often suffered from headaches, which Mary hoped mustard-seed and the constant use of hartshorn and exercise would cure, though the Duchess of Portland advocated a bit of stale bread about the size of a walnut to be eaten as soon as Anne woke. Earache, too, was a problem, and she stuffed her ears with black wool in an attempt to soothe the pain.

In the eighteenth century considerable reliance was put on the curing powers of the spas. Bath was the chief amongst them, and almost all Mary's friends and relatives went to Bath at some time in their lives for the purpose of improving their health. Bristol, Cheltenham and Tunbridge were also recommended. Evidently a little went a long way, for Mary wrote: 'I don't know the nature of Bristol waters – whether they require the same caution as the Bath.' Islington became popular towards the end of the century; Mary

wrote: 'Poor Lady Sunderland, who bears her misfortune with great strength of mind . . . goes constantly to Islington Wells, where she meets abundance of good company. These waters are rising in fame, and already pretend to vie with Tunbridge.'

On her return to London in 1733 Mary had settled in Lower Brook Street, where she was a close neighbour of George Frederick Handel. The great composer and impresario had settled in England in 1711 and had attained immense popularity with his operas among the aristocracy; at this time opera – in the Italian style – was one of the favourite forms of entertainment in fashionable society. Mary admired his music and always enjoyed his works above all others. Now he became a close family friend, particularly with her brother Bernard, who gave Handel two paintings by Rembrandt, which he later received back through a codicil to the composer's will.

One evening in 1734 Mary gave a musical party for thirteen friends, at which Handel and the famous soprano Strada (Anna Strada del Po), whom Handel had brought to London from Venice to sing in his operas, were guests. The party seems to have been a great success. Mary wrote:

Mr Handel was in the best humour in the world, and played lessons and accompanied Strada and all the ladies that sung from seven o'the clock till eleven. I gave them tea and coffee, and about half an hour after nine had a salver brought in of chocolate, mulled white wine and biscuits.

Calls were made to Handel's rooms to hear his rehearsals for new operas. On one occasion she listened to a new work, *Alcina*, four days before its first performance at Covent Garden. Her enthusiasm for this work knew no bounds: 'I think it the best he ever made, but I *have thought so* of *so many*, that I will not say positively *'tis the finest*, but 'tis *so fine* I have not words to describe it. Strada has a whole scene of charming recitative – there are a thousand beauties.'

Mary enjoyed to the full the best amusements that London's high society could offer, but she was also capable of taking an interest in more serious affairs. During the 1730s public sentiment had become increasingly inflamed by tales of harassment of the English merchant fleet by Spanish customs officials. The crisis came in 1739 with heated debates in Parliament demanding reprisals, and calls for war exciting the nation. Mary Pendarves had never been actively involved in politics, but on 3 March she wrote to Anne: 'Like a most noble patriot I have given up all private advantages for the good of my country.' Mary, in company with several other ladies, determined to attend the debates. On the first day they gained admission. Lady Mary Wortley Montagu, that outspoken and vociferous asserter of female liberty, described the invasion that ensued on the second day:

A tribe of dames resolved to show that neither men nor laws could resist them. These heroines were Lady Huntingdon, the Duchess of Queensbury, the Duchess of Ancaster, Lady Westmoreland, Lady Cobham, Lady Charlotte Edwin, Lady Archibald Hamilton and her daughter, Mrs Scott and Mrs Pendarves and Lady Francis Sanderson. I am thus particular in their names since I look upon them to be the boldest asserters and most resigned sufferers for liberty I have ever read of. They presented themselves at the door at nine o'clock in the morning, where Sir William Sanderson respectfully informed them that the Chancellor had made an order against their admittance. The Duchess of Queensbury, as head of the squadron, pished at the ill-breeding of a mere lawyer, and desired to let them upstairs privately. After some modest refusals, he swore by G— he would not let them in. Her Grace with a noble warmth, answered by G— they would come in, in spite of the Chancellor and the whole House. This being reported the Peers resolved to starve them out; an order was made that the doors should not be opened till they raised their siege. These Amazons now

A view inside the House of Commons, dated 1741, two years after Mary and her friends' dramatic invasion.

showed themselves qualified for the duty even of foot soldiers; they stood there till five in the afternoon, with neither sustenance nor evacuation, every now and then plying vollies of thumps, kicks, and raps against the door, with so much violence that the speeches in the House were scarce heard. When the Lords were not to be conquered by this, the two Duchesses (very well apprised of the use of stratagems in war) commanded a dead silence of half an hour; and the Chancellor, who thought this a certain sign of their absence, the Commons also being very impatient to enter, gave order for the opening of the door – upon which they all rushed in – pushed aside their competitors, and placed themselves in the front rows of the gallery. They stayed there till after eleven, when the House rose; and during the debates gave applause, and showed marks of dislike, not only by smiles and winks – which have always been allowed in these cases – but by noisy laughs and apparent contempts; which is supposed to be the true reason why poor Lord Hervey spoke miserably . . . You must own this action very well worthy of record, and I think not to be parallelled in history, ancient or modern.

In a letter to Anne, Mary Pendarves recounted her version of the event: 'My Lord Chesterfield spoke most exquisitely well – with *good sense, wit, and infinite spirit*! I never was so well entertained in my life . . .

Wellesbourne, the home of John and Anne Dewes.

much *circumfloribus* stuff was talked of on the Court side.' Her first-hand experience of the workings of government do not seem to have left Mary with a favourable impression of the world of politics: 'But enough of these affairs, those of friendship suit my nature better, where the struggles that arise are from very different principles than what animate courtiers and politicians, whose selfish views, under the glare of the good of their country, so often fill their hearts with a train of evil thoughts.'

In 1740 Mary was perturbed to learn of her sister's proposed marriage to Mr Dewes, a lawyer, of moderate income. His lineage, though not so illustrious as the Granvilles', was nevertheless considered suitably honourable. Discreet enquiries had been made by Anne's friend Lady Throckmorton of Mr Dewes' character, and the wedding took place in August of that year. This was to prove a happy and contented marriage in which Mr Dewes was increasingly liked and accepted by the family. Anne's marriage did not cause the sisters to become less close: on the contrary, Mary's family circle widened, and her advice was constantly sought on the upbringing of Anne's children.

Mary still showed no inclination to marry again, though she naturally had many admirers. Vivacious and attractive, artistic and intelligent, she combined virtue with a charm that endeared her to men and women alike. Throughout her nineteen years of widowhood she received many proposals, but her disastrous first marriage and her independent spirit made her wary of tying herself down. She had no romantic illusions about living happily ever after:

Amidst all the increases that matrimony may produce us, if ever we condescend to that state, we shall have no increase of happiness, *that I verily believe*; for in every state of life we have a share of sorrows in proportion to the pleasures dealt to us. I am not of the vulgar notion that fortune is so very partial.

John Wesley, the founder of the Methodists was greatly attracted to her; on one occasion as they walked over the Cotswold Hills together, he declared that the glory of her spirit threw a new brightness over the view. But his ideas and preaching were too radical for Mary. Of all her suitors it was Lord Baltimore towards whom she was most inclined. He 'fluttered' around her for five years but never actually proposed marriage to her and she was considerably distressed when she heard of his engagement and marriage in 1730. The invitation to stay in Ireland, which came shortly afterwards, was a welcome distraction: 'the real reason for my going was entirely locked within my own heart', Mary wrote.

From that visit to Ireland, however, her own married happiness was eventually to emerge, for Dr Delany had never forgotten Mary Pendarves, and when he was widowed in 1740 his thoughts turned to her. He was encouraged by Swift who assured him that Mary had several times asked to be remembered to him.

In April 1743 Dr Delany travelled to London, and wrote a letter of proposal to Mary from an inn at Dunstable. He was then fifty-eight and aware of his advancing years:

. . . however the vigour of my life may be over, and with that the *vigour of vanity*, and the flutter of passion, I find myself not less fitted for all that is solid happiness in the wedded state – the tenderness of affection and the faith of friendship.

I have a good clear income for my life; . . . a good house (as houses go in our part of the world), moderately furnished, a good many books, a pleasant garden (better I believe than when you saw it), etc. Would to God I might have leave to lay them all at your feet.

You will, I hope, pardon me the presumption of this wish, when I assure you it is no way blemished by the vanity of thinking them worthy of your acceptance, but as you have seen the vanities of the world to satiety, I allowed myself to indulge a hope that a retirement at this time of life, with a man whose turn of mind is not foreign from your own (and for that *only* reason not wholly unworthy of you) – a man who knows your worth, and honours you as much as he is capable of honouring any thing that is mortal, might not be altogether abhorrent from the views of your humble and unearthly wisdom.

Mary had been impressed by Dr Delany's good humour, his comfortable figure and his great love of nature; he was a devout Christian, whose mind and conversation she had found very agreeable. Her friend Mrs Montagu of Blue Stocking fame observed of Dr Delany: 'In his imagination I could see the poet, in his reflections the philosopher, and in both the divine.' Perhaps this was what Mary sought of matrimonial happiness: in any case, she indicated that, given the blessing of her family, she would accept him. Although Mary was now forty-three the conventions of the eighteenth century demanded that she should consider the views of her family.

It appears that Mary's mother and sister offered no objection, relying on Mary's judgement, but the men of the family were less amenable. Dr Patrick Delany was born the son of a servant to Sir John Russell, one of the Irish judges. His father had a small farm, and Patrick had won a sizarship at Trinity College, Dublin, where he took his degree and was elected a Fellow; he became one of the most popular tutors and celebrated preachers in the university. But in the eyes of the male Granvilles he was not born a gentleman, and no amount of learning on Delany's part could alter this. Lord Carteret, who as Lord Lieutenant of Ireland knew Delany well and liked him, could not agree to Delany marrying his cousin. Even Mary's kindly uncle, Sir John Stanley, who agreed that Mary must be allowed to make her own choice, was reticent about the marriage. But for her brother Bernard, who had grown into a somewhat crusty and snobbish bachelor, it was quite unacceptable for a Granville to marry one whose condition of birth was so different; Bernard considered it great presumption on Delany's part to have proposed. Days passed by as Mary considered the proposal and sought the agreement of her family. While Dr Delany waited anxiously for an answer, he pleaded with her to make up her own mind:

Where you *owe duty*, pay it; and let me rise or fall by the determination of *duty*; but let not the decision depend upon the fickle, the uncertain, and the selfish. God has blessed you with noble sentiments, a good understanding and a generous heart; are not these, under God, your best governors? I might venture to pronounce that even a parent has no right to control you, at this time of life, and under your circumstances, in opposition to these; and a *brother* has no shadow of right.

How much this last remark influenced Mary we do not know, but she finally consented, and early in June 1743 she was married to Patrick Delany.

'Lysimachia Vulgaris, Loosestrife'

4 *An Irish Idyll*

Dr Patrick Delany, Dean of Down.

Mary Delany from an enamel possibly by the painter, Barber, whose career she was eager to promote.

It is a measure of the leisurely pace of upper class life in the eighteenth century that the Delanys spent the first twelve months of their marriage in England visiting friends and relatives, before departing for Delville, Dr Delany's house in Dublin, where they arrived in June 1744. The twenty-five years of their marriage, spent mostly in Ireland with occasional visits to England, was to be a time of great happiness for Mary, and D.D., as she called him in her correspondence, was to prove a tender and devoted husband, giving Mary his constant affection and the encouragement to persevere in her artistic works. Swift described Dr Delany to Pope as 'a man of the easyest and best conversation I ever met with in this Island, a very good list'ner, a right reasoner, neither too silent, nor talkative, and never positive'. It was to be a comfortable marriage based on companionship rather than passion but the poem Dr Delany wrote comparing Mary to a rose shows the depth of his affection:

> O fairest emblem of the fair
> My pride, my life, my bliss, my care!
> Where all the lovelinesses meet –
> Beauty and grace, both bright and sweet!
> Emblem of Mary, gift divine.
> Blest be the hour that made her mine!

They shared their delight in the progress of their gardens at Delville and Downpatrick, they both enjoyed entertaining freely, and they concerned themselves with the welfare of their friends and the parishioners in the deanery.

One of their first duties after their arrival was to call on the Viceroy at Dublin Castle, which was the centre of Irish society – 'I dressed *in my airs* for formal visits' – and in return they received callers at Delville. There must have been many who remembered

Mary from her visit to Dublin thirteen years earlier, and who were keen to make her acquaintance again, surprised perhaps that the charming, talented and aristocratic widow, who must have had so many opportunities to marry a man of fortune, should have chosen an obscure, middle-aged Irish clergyman.

Mary's interest in clothes alerted her to the plight of the Irish traders resulting from the restrictions on the export of cloth: 'the poor weavers are starving, – all trade has met with a great check this year.' She decided that she must try and persuade the ladies who attended the frequent receptions at the Castle to have their dresses made of Irish cloth: 'Mrs Chenevix, the Bishop of Killaloe's wife, and I have agreed to go to the Birthday in Irish stuffs.' This apparently had the desired effect, because only three days later she wrote: 'On the Princess of Wales' birthday there appeared at Court a great number of Irish stuff, Lady Chesterfield (the Vicereign) was dressed in one, and I had the *secret satisfaction* of knowing myself to have been the cause, but *dare not say so here*; but I say "I am glad to find my Lady Chesterfield's example has had so good influence."'

Lt Hervey taking leave of his family, by Gravelot and others. This painting shows typical fashionable dresses of the mid-eighteenth century. The lady standing to the left wears a decorative apron. The seated lady has a 'rococo-style' border to her overskirt.

Mary was just the person to set this example because the other ladies, knowing that she had attended the very finest Court functions in England, were content to trust her good taste and follow her. How encouraged she must have been when at another royal birthday she noted 'It was prodigeously crowded, and all the ladies were dressed in Irish stuffs, and never looked finer or more genteel; except five or six who wore silk, and they were *not* distinguished to their honour. The men were not so public-spirited as the ladies – most of them were in their foreign finery.'

In middle-age Mary's comments on dress are less detailed and refer more to style and practicality, but are nevertheless interesting historically. When she attended a reception at Leicester House in 1747, during a visit to England, she wrote:

There was not much new finery, new clothes not being required on this Birthday, They curl and wear a great many *tawdry* things ... the only thing that seems general are hoops of an enormous size, and most people wear vast winkers to their heads. They are now come to such an extravagance in those two particulars, that I expect soon to see the other extreme of thread-paper heads and no hoops, and from appearing like so many *blown bladders* we shall look like so many *bodkins stalking about*.

The Delanys' main home was in Dublin, and they only paid annual visits to Downpatrick, seventy miles north of Dublin, where Dr Delany held the deanery; in those days a dean was not expected to move into the district to live among his parishioners. Soon after their arrival in Dublin they set out to make their first acquaintance of the deanery: 'The Dean and I travel in our chaise, which is easy and pleasant; Betty and Margaret, the cook and housemaid, in the coach and four, and Peg Hanages (who I am breeding up to be a housemaid) in a car we have had made for marketing, and carrying luggage, &c, when we travel.' They took with them linen, china, and similar domestic items, packed in hay by the servants, whom she referred to as 'the family'.

For a while they occupied a house called Holly Mount, before moving to another named Mount Panther, which was nearer the town of Down. It was a shock to them both to find how the parishioners had been neglected by the curate left in charge:

Never did any flock want more the presence and assistance of a shepherd than this Deanery, where there has been a most *shameful neglect*; and I trust in God it will be a very happy thing for the poor people that D.D. is come among them. The church of Down is very large, but it is *not a quarter* filled with people; the Curate has been so negligent as *never to visit any of the poor* of

'A view of Hollymount in the road to Down Patrick', detail of a sketch by Mrs Delany, 1745.

the parish, and a very diligent and watchful dissenting preacher has visited them on all occasions of sickness and distress, and by that means gained great numbers to the meetings. D.D. has already visited a great number, when he has been with all the *Protestants* he designs to go to the *Presbyterians*, and *then to the Papists*, they bless him and pray for him wherever he goes, and say he has done more good already than all his predecessors; the last Dean was here but *two days* in *six years*!

Dr Delany's appointment as Dean of Downpatrick had been achieved through Mary's family connections with Lord Carteret, then Prime Minister. Indeed, most appointments in both church and state came from private patronage. There could be great disparity in the position of clergymen: some of the bishops were wealthy and influential men, especially those who had married an heiress, whereas a curate might earn as little as forty pounds per annum.

Mary enjoyed her visits to the deanery, where life was simple and rural. She and the Dean created a new garden round Holly Mount, went for walks in the fields looking for new plants, and met the local people.

This is really a sweet place, the house *ordinary* but is well enough for a *summer house* . . . four pretty good bed-chambers, and a great many conveniences for the servants . . . I have a closet to my bedchamber, the window of which looks upon a fine lake *inhabited* by *swans*, beyond it and on each side are pretty hills, some covered with wood and others with cattle.

It is with the eye of an artist and a needlewoman that Mary describes the scene: 'In some places a view of the lake opens, and most of the trees are embroidered with woodbine and the "*flaunting eglantine*".' The following week when she was still in the process of describing her new abode to Anne she wrote:

As soon as dinner was over we walked to Wood Island, where the Dean amused himself with his workmen, and I at my work under the shelter of a young oak in which D.D. had made a very snug seat. When he had discharged his labourers we set forward for adventures; and as bold as Don Quixote, he undertook, armed with a stout cane instead of a lance, and I (with my shepherdess's crook) followed intrepid, to penetrate the thickest part of the wood, where human foot *had not* trod *I believe for ages*. After magnanimously combating brakes, briars, and fern of *enormous size* and thickness, we accomplished the arduous task, and were well rewarded during our toil by finding many pretty spots enamelled and perfumed with variety of sweet flowers, particularly the *woodbine and wild rose*.

A typical day at Holly Mount was described by Mary:

We rise about seven, have prayers and breakfast over by nine. In the

A typical indoor eighteenth-century scene. One lady is reading, while her companion twists thread. A silhouette cut by Mrs Delany.

mornings D.D. makes his visits, I draw; when it is fair and he walks out I go with him; we dine at two; in the afternoon when we can't walk out, reading and talking amuse us till supper, and after supper I make shirts and shifts for the poor naked wretches in the neighbourhood.

They lost no time in getting to know the people of Down, and announced that Tuesdays would be their 'public days', which meant they were at home to anyone who wished to call. So that they might be less rushed on Sundays, they arranged to dine at a public-house in Down kept by a former butler of one of the Deans: '. . . he has a very good room in his house, and he is to provide a good dinner, and the Dean will fill his table every Sunday with all the townsmen and their wives *by turns*, which will oblige the people, and give us an opportunity of going to church in the afternoon without any fatigue.'

The Delanys frequently entertained at home and the following meal for twelve was typical: 'Our dinner was a boiled leg of mutton, a sirloin of roast beef, six boiled chickens, bacon and greens; apple-pies, a dish of potatoes.' Sometimes at Mount Panther, which was larger, as many as twenty would sit down to dinner, and considerable good management of the household was necessary, for we read: 'On Tuesday sixteen people here at dinner, on Wednesday ten, on Thursday twenty-two'. The younger generation was entertained to small 'drums'; Mary was a keen match-maker and any eligible young man was noted:

Mr Cole (five thousand a year and just come from abroad) a pretty, well-behaved young man . . . Miss Bayly was queen of the ball, and began it with Mr Cole . . . there were ten couple of clever dancers. Remember my

room is 32 feet long; at the upper end sat the fiddlers, and at the lower end next the little parlour the lookers-on. Tea from seven to ten: it was made in the hall, and Smith [her personal maid] presided. They began at *six* and *ended at ten*; then went to a cold supper in the drawing-room made of 7 dishes down the middle of different cold dishes, and plates of all sorts of fruit and sweet things that could be had here, in the middle jellies.

Though Mary delighted in the generous hospitality of the Irish there are occasions when she thought it too lavish:

Last Tuesday we dined at the Bishop of Elphin's . . . we had a magnificent dinner, extremely well drest and well attended, nine and nine, and a dessert the finest I ever saw in Ireland; the Bishop lives constantly very well, and it becomes his station and fortune, but *high living is too much the fashion here*. You are invited to dinner to any private gentleman of a £1000 a year or less, that does not give you seven dishes at one course, and Burgundy and Champagne; and these dinners they give once or twice a week, that provision is now as dear as in London . . . I own I am surprised *how* they manage; for we cannot afford anything like it, with a *much better income*.

Similar disapproval is expressed when they dine with the Primate and have a Périgord pie, sent from France: 'such expensive rarities *do not become the table of a prelate*; who ought rather *to be given hospitality*, than ape the fantastical luxuriances of fashionable tables.'

Unexpected guests were invited to stay for dinner in surprising numbers and must have stretched the ingenuity of the cook, but joints of meat were large and succulent and the menus generous:

66

They (Dr Mathews and his family) were all the company I *expected*, but there were added to them by dinner-time, Mr Johnston, a very good sort of man (agent, that is rent-gatherer to the Dean); his wife and niece, both *fine ladies*!; the sheriff of the county; and *three persons* of very different characters – Mr Hall, a crafty mercenary man, not at all esteemed or countenanced by the good people of this country; Mr Ward, a plain honest curate, and Mr Cornabee, a Frenchman by birth, who has a living in the neighbourhood – a polite, lively, entertaining man, just come from the Queen of Hungary.

In middle-age Mary tended to become more conservative and regretted change – a trait commonly acquired with increasing years. She deplored innovations in the social customs of local people in Down:

I am very sorry to find here and everywhere people *out of character*, and that *wine* and *tea* should enter where they have *no pretence to be*, and usurp the rural food of syllabub . . . The dairymaids wear large hoops and velvet hoods instead of the round *tight petticoat* and *straw hat*, and there is as much foppery introduced in the food as in the dress, – the *pure simplicity of ye country is quite lost*!

Mary was very interested in botany and was always on the look-out for new plants, whether she was taking a short walk or making a journey of several miles. Wherever she went she liked to examine the plants closely and she picked out the details which enabled her to

This satirical print of 1760 echoes Mary's sentiments towards the changing country manners. A farmer's daughter returns from Dublin; her towering hairstyle has been caught in a farming implement hanging from the ceiling.

create such realistic designs in her needlework. She describes a little walk with her god-daughter Sally Chapone, daughter of her childhood friend Sarah Kirkham:

Sally and I grumble a little at the weather, which prevents us going among the *herbs and flowers* to find out some that may be rare to you. There grows a little pale purple aster, with a yellow thrum (very like the *asterattims*), in all the borders near the lakes and sea. *Matfellon* and *figwort* flourish here remarkably, and the purple vetch and eyebright soften the golden furs, and glowing heath. A poetical pen might have done their beauties justice.

Sometimes there were more adventurous walks and picnics: 'According to the country phrase, yesterday Sally and I *fetched* a charming walk at least six miles! We set out at a quarter after ten with bags and baskets to store our curiosities in.'

Mary was not content just to admire the beauty of the plants: she also wanted to know all about them and had her botany books at hand. On a hot August day in 1763 she wrote: 'Sally and I saunter abroad a good deal in the cool part of the day, bring home handfuls of wild plants and search for their names and virtues in Hill – but he is not half so intelligible as old Gerard.'

'A View of the salt water Lake near Down Patrick in Ireland', a sketch by Mary Delany. Mary enjoyed the summers at Down Patrick, and spent many happy hours exploring the countryside.

RIGHT 'Æscalus Hippocastanum, Horse Chestnut': I have bungled out a horse chestnut blossom.'

OVERLEAF
LEFT 'Mespilus piracantha' [*Pyracantha coccinea*]. Mrs Delany was 80 years old when she worked this flower; RIGHT 'Lilium canadense' [*Lilium superbum*], showing 6 stamens and 1 style (Hexandria Monogynia).

LEFT 'Passeflora Laurifolia, Bay Leaved'. There are over 230 paper petals in the bloom.

In September 1758 the Delanys and Sally set out for a visit to the Giant's Causeway staying with friends on the way. They travelled in 'a train of two chaises and two cars with us, Mr Bayly and Mr Mathew, one of D.D.'s curates, on horseback, and our sumpter-car. From Mount Panther to Ballanehinch (7 miles) is the rudest country I ever saw – rough hills, mountains, and bogs, but some of them covered with furze in blossom, heath, and thyme.' They arrived at the Causeway in a coach drawn by six horses, lent them while their own were resting and, uncharacteristically, Mary seems unable to find words to describe the scene: 'I am now quite at a loss to give you an idea of it; it is so different from anything I ever saw.' They proceeded along a precipitous path which 'led us a great way about, and was so frightful that we could not look about us'. Likening the rock formations to three amphitheatres, she continued:

This third amphitheatre contains the greatest quantity of the pillars, some so very exact and smooth that you would imagine they were all chiselled with the greatest care. After gazing, wondering, and I may say *adoring* the wondrous Hand that formed this amazing work, we began to find ourselves fatigued. Our gentlemen found out a well-sheltered place, where we sat very commodiously by a well (called the Giant's Well).

There they picnicked on cold mutton and tongue after a walk of three hours. Out came Mary's sketch-book and pencil to record this strange upheaval of nature; her verbal sketch to Anne continues:

Whilst we were at our repast our attendants were differently grouped, at some distance along the left hand the servants, a little below us the women and children that gathered sea-weed and shells for us, about twelve in number with very little drapery; on the right hand men that were our guides of different ages, seated on the points of the rocks, whose figures were *very droll*, and I believe we ourselves were no less so; eagerly devouring our morsel, and every now and then a violent exclamation of wonder at some new observation. We sat just facing a most aspiring pyramidal hill, and whilst we were there a shepherd drove his flocks to the summit of it, and they looked like as many little white specks; the shepherd stood for some minutes on the highest point of the rocks.

It was a memorable day only slightly clouded by the Dean's shin becoming inflamed after a nasty graze some days earlier, but it was soon healed by the application of Turner's cerate.

Throughout their absence from each other Mary was consulted and kept informed by Anne of family affairs in England. Anne Dewes was living at Wellesbourne, Warwickshire and now had a

Sally Chapone, Mary's god-daughter, who lived with the Delanys in Ireland.

73

family of three boys and a girl, and Mary regularly gave advice on the upbringing of her nephews and niece. On the matter of employing a nurse, she warned: 'a deaf nurse is not to be endured; thè poor dear may make his little moans, and have a thousand uneasinesses that she will hear nothing of.'

'The Rocky Hills and Mountains leading to the Giant's Causeway in the County of Antrim, Ireland', a sketch by Mary Delany.

Mary was particularly anxious about the upbringing of her niece:

I *cannot* think it necessary to the accomplishment of a young lady that she should be *early* and *frequently* produced in public, and I should rather see a little awkward bashfulness, than a *daring and forward genteelness*! Good company and good conversation I should wish to have my niece introduced into as soon as she can speak and understand, but for all public places till *after fifteen* (except a play or oratorio) she should not know what they are, and then *very rarely*, and *only* with her mother or aunt. I believe you and I are perfectly well agreed on these points, and I am sure the general behaviour of the young people will not encourage us to alter our scheme. I think all public water-drinking places *more pernicious* than a masquerade, and *that* I have *not* a *very good* opinion of.

A warning is given that her niece should not be led astray by her own good looks:

If Mary proves handsome . . . it is vain to hope that she can be kept *ignorant of it*; all that the wisest friend can do for her is to teach her how little value

74

beauty is – how few years it lasts – how liable to be tarnished, and if it has its advantages, what a train of inconveniences also attend it; that it requires a double portion of discretion to guard it, and much more caution and restraint, than one who is not handsome. Beauty where there is a beam of light to show the virtues of the mind is a blessing to be wished for, but if its allurements *only* discover *folly and sin*, it is a *curse indeed*!

To emphasise this point Mary wrote to her niece when she was only nine years old: 'the graces of the mind will shine when those of the person decay – and are therefore worth more care.'

Discipline was considered by her to be an important ingredient for happiness, and she thought parents should be in complete control of their children:

'I think all public water-drinking places *more pernicious* than a masquerade, and *that* I have *not* a *very good* opinion of.' This satire shows a lady returning from a masquerade.

An *early obedience* saves an infinite chagrins to parents and children, and a very little experience must teach us that the most wretched beings are those who have no command of their passions, and *that foundation* must be laid very early, and may be done so cautiously as hardly to be perceived by the little pupil till it gains such ground as to become a habit.

Mary encourages Anne in meting out suitable punishment to her children, including the use of birch twigs: 'I think you have exerted the motherly authority very heroically and I don't doubt but he will bless you in time for the *little smart* he has received from your hands.'

When Mary Dewes was six years old a young gentlewoman was employed to teach her plain needlework and to progress later to fine linen and laces, and to teach good manners. 'I am much pleased with your account of Charlotte Herbert; those gentle refined manners are very desirable; they accustom children betimes to civility, and when they have it not in their nursery they are apt to fly out in the parlour and drawing-room.'

Nowadays when so many minor ailments can be cured by easily obtained proprietary ointments or medicines, it is difficult to imagine what it must have been like to be unwell in an age when there was very little free medical care, particularly in the country districts where physicians were few and far between. Many concocted their own recipes, which if thought to be efficacious would be passed on from one to the other. From Mary's pen we hear of a cure for coughing that had afflicted her niece:

Two or three snails boiled in her barley-water, or tea-water, or whatever she drinks, might be of great service to her; taken in time they have done *wonderful cures* – she must know nothing of it – they give no manner of taste. It would be best nobody should know it but yourself, and I should imagine 6 or 8 boiled in a quart of water strained off and put into a bottle, adding a spoonful or two of that to *every liquid* she takes. They must be fresh done every 2 or 3 days, otherwise they grow too thick.

Some of the recommended prescriptions seem very drastic; when Bernard Dewes, as a young child, was unwell, Mary wrote: 'I am told by a very wise woman, that quick-silver-water is the most effectual remedy for worms that can be taken, and must be continued constantly for a year together, and the elixir may be taken at times. A pound of quick-silver boiled in a gallon of water till half the water is consumed away to be constantly drank at his meals, or whenever he is dry.' When Court Dewes was about two years old Anne was advised:

Meat should now be given three times a week and pudding and panada the other days. Sometimes sheeps totters [sic] which are both innocent and nourishing. Make him to be jumbled about a good deal for fear of falling into rickets, and throw away his wormwood draughts, for they signify nothing for an ague. Have attention to him about worms which are the cause of most children's illness.

Mary's continuing interest in Anne's children and her frequent offers of advice do not seem to have caused any offence; indeed Anne recognised and valued her sister's wisdom. Mary was a shrewd judge of character, and was astute enough to recognise her own failings: 'We create the greatest part of our miseries by the uneasiness of our own tempers. I never had one to vex me extremely, but when it was over, and I have examined the cause of it strictly, I have been convinced I had no reason for half the unhappiness I had felt.'

Mary moved in the leading ranks of society, yet skilfully managed to avoid the pitfalls of the '*beau monde*'. She enjoyed life to its full, and in 1752 wrote with charming frankness: 'Though I do not love money for its own sake I love to spend it', but she was at the same time aware of the over-emphasis on material values which could bring so much unhappiness. Throughout her life her deeply-held religious beliefs lent her a serenity and confidence that are reflected in her words and her work. She was convinced that life after death would bring greater joy than life on earth. In the same year she expressed surprise at:

... the horror that most people have of dying, so that instead of preparing them-selves for an event that must come, they drive the thought away as far as they can, not considering how much more dreadful that must make the fatal hour when it arrives. Amongst the numberless mercies of God, surely none is greater than the *gradual* weaning us from the world, which everybody that lives rationally must be sensible of. A strong desire of living and enjoying the world is implanted in us; without it we could not support the thousand shocks we meet with in our progress; but as years increase upon us, that desire lessens; we see how transient and unsatisfactory most of our pursuits and enjoyments are; we feel that our perfect happiness cannot be made out in this life, and that perfect joys are reserved for another!

Of attendance at church she wrote: 'Of all our mutual employments none can give us so much satisfaction as that in which we have just been engaged; and through the tender mercies of God, it may be the means of our meeting where we shall never more be separated.'

Whenever possible the Delanys drove into Dublin to attend

concerts in aid of charities. At this time some of the notable hospitals were being built. Amongst them was the Lying-In Hospital, founded by the physician Dr Mosse. Funds depended on the profits of these concerts given in the great gardens behind the buildings, where the finest singers from Europe sang in the Rotunda. In an attempt to encourage more subscribers to his list, Dr Mosse organised a free breakfast together with a concert. The Delanys, who were keen to hear the music, went along, but the lure of a free breakfast drew large crowds which evidently had no intention of subscribing. Later, in the evening, the Delanys recalled the events of the day as a 'matter of mirth', as she describes to Anne:

The music allured us . . . and with some difficulty we squeezed into the room which is 60 feet long, and got up to the breakfast-table which had been well pillaged; but the fragments of cakes, bread and butter, silver coffee pots, and tea kettles without number, and all sorts of spring flowers strewed on the table, shewed it had been set out plentifully and elegantly. The company indeed looked as if their principal design of coming was for breakfast. When they had satisfied their hunger the remains were taken away, and such torrent of rude mob (for they deserved no better name) *crowded in* that I and my company *crowded out* as fast as we could, glad we escaped in whole skins, and resolving never more to add to the throng of *gratis* entertainments. We got away with all speed, without hearing a note of the music . . .

Any music by Handel was a special delight to them: 'Last Monday the Dean and I went to the rehearsal of the Messiah, for the relief of poor debtors.' This oratorio was first performed in Dublin in April 1742, when Mrs Cibber, sister of Dr Arne, sang with such feeling that Dr Delany is said to have exclaimed: 'Woman for this, be all thy sins forgiven.'

Not all concerts were so well received, however, and an eighteenth-century audience could be quite ruthless in their treatment of any performer who failed to please. Mary describes a concert given by the eminent though elderly composer, Francesco Geminiani, of his own works, which she attended with the Duchess of Bedford, the Lady Lieutenant, and a small party:

The music began at half an hour after seven; I was extremely pleased with it; there is a spirit of harmony and prettiness of fancy which no other music (beside our dear Handel's) has. He played one of his own solos most wonderfully well for a man of eighty-six years of age, and one of his fingers hurt; but the sweetness and melody of the tone of the fiddle, his fine and elegant taste, and the perfection of *time and tune* made full amends for some failures in his play occasioned by the weakness of his hand; and his clever management of passages too difficult for him to execute with the spirit he used to do was very surprising. On the whole I was greatly entertained, though it is the fashion to shrug up the shoulders and say '*poor old man*' with impertinent etceteras. I felt *quite peevish* at their remarks. The great ladies and their attendant peers were so impatient to get to *their cards* and to their dancing, that a message was sent to Geminiani to '*shorten the musical entertainment*'. I was quite provoked, the concert was not above one hour: I could have sat three hours more with pleasure to have heard it. I have invited Geminiani to come and see me and hope to hear this music some way or other.

There were other social gatherings with entertainment on a flamboyant scale. Mary described one such entertainment arranged by Lord Belfield, their step son-in-law:

. . . the *room represents a wood* . . . at one end is a portico on Doric pillars, lighted by baskets of flowers, the candles *green wax*, so that nothing appears but the flame . . . from the portico to the end of the stage is diversified by rocks, trees and caves, very well represented . . . a jessamine bower, a Gothic temple, (which is to be the sideboard) trees interspersed, the whole terminates with a grotto extremely well exprest; three rustick arches, set off with ivy, moss, icicles, and all the rocky appurtances; the musicians to be placed in the grotto dressed like shepherds and shepherdesses . . . the trees are *real trees* with *artificial leaves*, but when all is done it will be too much crowded to be agreeable, and most dangerous if a spark of a candle should fall on any of the scenery, which is all painted paper!

The arrangements for providing refreshments seem to have been as original as the decor: 'If tea, coffee, or chocolate were wanting, you held your cup to a leaf of a tree, and it was filled; and whatever you wanted to eat or drink was immediately found on a rock, or on a branch, or in the hollow of a tree, the waiters were all in whimsical dress . . .' Naturally, such an extravagant show could not please all: '. . . a few dissenters have the assurance to say, it was no better than a poppet-show.'

Gardens and their lay-outs continued to be one of Mary Delany's chief interests, and no opportunity was lost to visit and comment upon them:

Today we dine at Lord Chief Justic Singleton's at Drumcondra. He has given Mr Bristowe *full dominion* over house and gardens, and like a conceited connoisseur he is doing *strange things* building an absurd room, turning fine wild evergreens *out of the garden, cutting down*, full grown elms and *planting twigs*! D.D. has no patience with him, and I shall be under some difficulty today to know *how* to commend *anything*, which is what I wish to do.

She had firm ideas on what was acceptable in landscaping, and strict aesthetic requirements. She would have nothing to do with 'virtuoso epicuroso' improvements, such as Mr Bristowe had carried out in his 'conceit', yet she appreciated the charming fancies of Lord Orrery, Pope's friend at Caledon, Co. Tyrone, where he had been planting and landscaping extensively in a style much influenced by Pope's Twickenham (a style that had influenced Dr Delany too). She was intrigued by the hermit's root-house with pebble floor. Inside, on a wooden table, were placed a manuscript, a pair of spectacles, a leather bottle, an hour glass, and mathematical instruments; there was a shelf of books, wooden platters and bowls and a couch of matting completed the imaginary hermit's cultural and practical needs. This was acceptable because it did not interfere with nature, but was a terminal point in a walk around his house taking in a series of gardens, including an orchard, a flower-garden, a physic garden, and a kitchen garden: '. . . I never saw so pretty a *whim* so *thoroughly well* executed.' Mary was also interested in commenting upon the owners:

Orrery is *more agreeable* than he used to be; he has laid aside the ceremonious stiffness that was a great disadvantage to him. He is very well-bred and entertaining; his lady (whose fortune was near 3000 pounds a year), is very plain in her person and manner, but to make amends for that she is very sensible, unaffected, good humoured, and obliging.

Many eighteenth-century hosts enjoyed entertaining and showing their guests their newly landscaped estates. Mary's description of their visit to Lord Hillsborough's gives a glimpse of such a party, which of course, included the inevitable tour round the garden.

Lord Hillsborough is very well bred, sensible and entertaining, and nothing could be more polite that he was to all his company. Sally and I being the only women, we had the principal share of his address; he is handsome and genteel . . . we were twelve in company . . . Lord Hillsborough was very merry and said a great many lively and comical things . . . After the ladies had given their toasts they were desired to '*command the house*'; the hint was taken and I said I would upon that liberty go and prepare the tea-table for the gentlemen. Sally and I took a little step out into the garden to look at the prospect, but the weather soon drove us back. Candles lighted, tea-table and gentlemen soon came together. I made the tea. Cribbage was proposed, and I consented to be of the party, thinking it would be some relief to Lord Hillsborough; at ten we went to supper, at eleven to bed; met at nine the next morning at breakfast.

In spite of recent rain which deterred some of the party, Mary, who was not so easily dissuaded, accompanied her host round his park to

The park at Longleat as landscaped by Capability Brown, from Humphrey Repton's 'Red Book' for Longleat, which contained Repton's proposed changes.

see 'the improvements, a gravel path two Irish miles long, the ground laid out in very good taste, some wood, some nurseries; shrubs and flowers diversify the scene; a pretty piece of water with an island in it, and all the views pleasant.'

Their travels around England gave them welcome opportunities to see for themselves examples of landscaping by Capability Brown, of whom they had heard so much. While the Delanys were staying at Bath in 1760 for the Dean to take the waters, Mary visited Longleat. She was amazed to note:

There is not much alteration in the house, *but the gardens are no more*! They are succeeded by a fine lawn, a serpentine river, wooded hills, gravel paths meandering round a shrubbery *all modernised* by the ingenious Mr Brown! There are schemes for further improvements . . . Lady Weymouth carried Miss Chapone and me all over the park, and shewed us the menagerie; I never saw such a quantity of gold pheasants; they turn them wild into the woods in hopes of breeding there.

On passing Lord Cornbury's estate near Burford Mary wrote:

After a good breakfast of caudle we set forward for Cornbury, and sent a messenger forward to ask leave to go through the park, and to say if my Lord Cornbury was alone we would breakfast with him; he sent back an invitation to us to dine as well as breakfast, and entertained us with

A contemporary print shows the Duke of Cumberland leading his troops against the rebel Jacobites.

showing us his house, pictures, and park . . . his house lies finely to the park and is most charming, and kept as nice as a garden, and a gravel path quite round it, that you may walk in any weather. The ground lies most advantageously and is planted with great skill and great variety of fine trees, some thick wood, some clumps, in short nature and art have done their best to make it beautiful.

The practical side of the estates that they visited interested her too:

Thursday spent the day at Castle Wellan, Mr Annesley's, and walked two or three miles before dinner, saw all his farming affairs, which are indeed very fine. Three large courts; round the first, which is arched round a kind of piazza, are houses for all his carriages, and over them his granaries; the next court are stables and cow-houses, and over them haylofts; the third court two such barns as I never saw, *floored with oak*, and finished in the most convenient manner for the purposes of winnowing.

She was equally impressed at the unsophisticated scene beside a salmon-leap on the river Liffey when she and the Dean called on Mr and Mrs Law at their bleachyard: 'They have a pretty cabin there, and gave us some fine trout caught out of their own brook just at their door . . . it was so new a scene . . . the men at work laying out the cloth &c on the grass full in our view was very pretty; the machine for rinsing the clothes is very curious.'

As always, Mary kept herself informed on the events of the day.

The political turmoils of the time also feature in her letters. When, on his way to Derby in 1745, the Young Pretender, Bonnie Prince Charlie, invaded England from Scotland his army passed close to Calwich on the Staffordshire border, where her brother Bernard lived. In December Mary wrote in a state of alarm from Ireland: 'Many flying reports we have had of the entire defeat of the rebels . . . the rumour of one day is to be contradicted by the next . . . I had terrified myself extremely on his account; I could not think of him surrounded by those desperate rebels without fearing the worst that could happen.' But Bernard was safe with Anne at Gloucester. The war with the French also brought worries. On 14 February 1758 Mary wrote of Colonel Clive's victory at Plassey in India: 'Glorious news come today of Clive's victory. He shames all our generals.' The battle had in fact, taken place in June of the previous year; it had taken eight months for the news to travel by ship round the Cape of Good Hope. Two years later Ireland was threatened with invasion and in November 1759 we find the Delanys thinking of economies: 'We determined to go to the Birthday, but hearing so much said of the *intended invasion*, on our return home (D.D.) resolved against it as an unnecessary expense at a time when money may prove very scarce; I hope the alarm will prove nothing.' Four months later the threat appears to have receded: 'We are all joy and transport at the taking of three French ships . . . we are now, thank *God* restored to a peaceful state in *this kingdom*, and I wish the peace were more universal.'

5 *Pleasures and Pastimes*

The years spent at Delville were to be one of the happiest periods of Mary Delany's life. It was the first house she could truly call her own, for she had felt no love for the houses she had shared with Mr Pendarves. At Delville she had not only a lovely home but the constant affection, companionship and encouragement of Dr Delany.

The garden was a mutual joy. She was enchanted by the new style of natural gardening that Dr Delany had followed at Delville. He and Swift had stayed at Twickenham with Alexander Pope whose landscaped garden was to set a new fashion, succeeding the formal and Dutch style that had prevailed in Great Britain and on the Continent for so long. It appears likely that Dr Delany had been impressed by Pope's ideas, for Delville was one of the first Irish gardens to be designed after nature.

On seeing her new home Mrs Delany wrote to her sister in July 1744 as enthusiastically as any bride:

I wish I could give you an idea of our garden, but the describing it puzzles me extremely; the back part of the house is towards a bowling-green, that slopes gently off down to a little brook that runs through the garden; on the other side of the brook is a high bank with a hanging wood of evergreens at the top of which is a circular terrace that surrounds the greatest part of the garden, the wall of which is covered with fruit trees, and on the other side of the wall a border for flowers and the greatest quantity of roses and sweet briar that ever I saw; on the right hand of the bowling-green is placed our hayrick, which is at present making, and from our parlour window and bedchamber I can see the men work at it . . . These fields are planted in a *wild way with forest-trees and with bushes*, that look so naturally you would not imagine it the work of art . . . a very good kitchen-garden and two fruit-gardens which . . . will afford us sufficient quantity of every thing we can want of that kind. There are several prettinesses I can't explain to you – little wild walks, private seats, and lovely prospects. One seat

'A view of Delville from beyond the Ever-Green Grove', drawn by Letitia Bushe, August 1754.

particularly I am very fond of in a nut grove, and the beggar's hut which is a seat in a rock . . . is placed at the end of a cunning wild path, the brook . . . entertains you with a purling rill. The little robins are as fond of this seat as we are; it just holds the Dean and myself, and I hope in God to have many a tete-a-tete there with my own dear sist^r.

'A view of ye Beggars Hut in Delville garden', a drawing by Mrs Delany.

Mrs Delany's constant hope was that Anne should come and spend part of a summer with them at Delville, though this was never realised. However, in March 1746 we find her looking forward to seeing Anne in England on their impending visit:

Our garden is now a wilderness of sweets. The violets, sweet briar, and primroses perfume the air, and the thrushes are full of melody and make our concert complete. It is the pleasantest music I have heard this year, and refreshes my spirits without the alloy of a tumultuous crowd, which attends all the other concerts. Two robins and one chaffinch fed off D.D.'s hand as we walked together this morning. I have been planting sweets in my 'Pearly Bower'–honeysuckles, sweet briar, roses and jessamine to climb up the trees that compose it, and for the carpet, violets, primroses and cowslips. This year I shall not smell their fragrance, nor see their bloom, but I shall see the dear person to whom the bower is dedicated, I hope, and I think I shall not repine at the exchange.

86

A ninepin alley was planned which Mrs Delany described as 'a very merry exercise', but through all these schemes they were careful to keep the natural look, and used sheep to close-crop their lawns. 'We had thoughts of having a bowling-green before our house in the garden front; but the hill, which descends gradually to the brook, looks so natural and pretty as it is, that it would be a pity to make it level; and so we are determined to keep it a lawn, and to have sheep.'

It was usually a pleasure to Mrs Delany to show her friends and acquaintances round the garden, and she wrote proudly of the interest taken by Lord and Lady Chesterfield: 'We went into the garden and walked over every inch of it; they seemed much surprised by the variety they found there, and could not have said more civil things had it been my Lord Cobham's Stowe!' But she was distinctly disappointed at the lack of appreciation shown by Lady Bell Monck 'no eyes nor understanding to see *that it was not a common vulgar garden*, and she did not commend anything she saw.'

In the summer months a large part of the day was often spent in the garden. Mrs Delany liked to breakfast outside, sitting in the shade of her nut trees in the grove of elms and listening to music played by a harper concealed in the trees. The day was spent in shell-work, needlework, painting and drawing, and she would walk among her animals to see they were properly cared for. Sometimes they drank tea in the orangerie, then wandered over the meadows to feed the deer and watch the cows being milked. On returning to the

'A view of y.ᵉ cold Bath field in Delville Garden', a drawing by Mrs Delany.

house books were read aloud, enabling Mrs Delany to keep up to date with new literature while continuing her 'candle-light work'. Prayers at eight were followed by music till supper, then a pool of commerce if there were guests in the house.

Although she enjoyed the occasional 'sweet solitary day', Mrs Delany made a point of entertaining at home and going into society for she felt it was 'a duty incumbent on us to live sociably, and it is necessary to keep up good humour and benevolence in ourselves, or the qualities of the heart contract and grow useless, as our limbs would do without proper exercise.' Her real pleasure, though, came in her many creative activities, which flourished in the warmth of her husband's admiration:

His approving of my works, and encouraging me to go on, keep up my relish to them, and make them more delightful to me than assemblies, plays, or an opera would be without he shared them with me. *Eager* as I am in all my pursuits, I am *easily checked and the least disapprobation or snap*, from the person I wish to oblige, in thought, word, or deed, would soon give me a distaste to what was delightful to me before! I hope this does not proceed from pride, but from a disposition in my heart that will not suffer me to enjoy any pleasure that I cannot communicate.

She turned her skill in needlework to the delightful task of making furnishings for her new home. She made covers for her drawing-room chairs, one set for summer and another for winter. The winter covers were made of worsted chenille, each one embroidered with a different group of flowers, while those for summer use were in brilliant blue linen, decorated with husks and leaves in white linen, sewn down with five varieties of knotting. The set was in perfect condition a hundred years later in spite of repeated washings.

For the chapel, too, furnishings were required: 'I am working coverings for the seats in chenille on a black ground, which gives it a gravity . . . My pattern a border of *oak-branches and all sorts of roses* (except yellow), which I work without any pattern, just as they come into my head.' It is surprising, in view of her belief that the beauties of nature were all God-given, to find Mrs Delany writing two months later: 'I have laid aside my scheme of the *roses* for my chapel cushions as too gay for the purpose, and have set all hands to work to finish some crimson double cross-stitch in diamonds which looks rich and grave.'

She worked a quilt and a coverlet. As long as four hours at a time were spent working at the quilt, which she began in 1747, and which was still receiving her attention three years later. It was composed of

One of the summer covers of Mrs Delany's drawing-room chairs, from an album of 19th-century photographs.

RIGHT A coverlet of white linen worked by Mrs Delany for her god-son, Thomas Sandford, son of Sally Chapone (later Mrs Sandford).

white Indian cotton lined with linen, bordered with flowers from nature, and bows of ribbon, with groups at the corners and centre of each side made with running stitches; the centre of the quilt had an intricate mosaic pattern of white knotting. The coverlet, now in the Ulster Museum, Belfast, was probably worked in the 1760s as a gift to her godson Thomas Sandford. It is composed of knotting and couched cord on white linen, the whole in monochrome. There is a central medallion of leaves intermingled with stylised flower heads, surrounded by a square border of leaves, with a trellis design covering most of the remainder of the quilt.

For her personal attire and that of her friends she made aprons, which had a purely decorative use in the eighteenth century. One was in heavy silk embroidered with purple and white violets and leaves in hard twisted silks. Another of black silk had a border of auriculas and geraniums. Handkerchiefs, which formed the top of a bodice and went round the neck, were also embroidered with flowers. On one tiffany handkerchief she introduced poppies, a particular favourite, and other flowers linked with bows of blue ribbon, the flowers delineated and shaded in running stitches. Another handkerchief bordered with flowers had Madonna lilies in the corner.

One of her greatest masterpieces in needlework was her own court dress which she designed and worked on black silk. It is typical of the style of the mid-eighteenth century, with its stomacher forming the front bodice, an over-skirt with a superb rococo border, and a petticoat which fronts the skirt. Though the dress was cut up and framed about one hundred and thirty years ago the skirt and petticoat are largely intact. An album of her drawings has shown that she drew many of the larger flowers first, occasionally making small alterations to the design when working the embroidery. The stomacher, of which there is now only a faded photograph, was of black velvet, with silk lace and embroidery, a line of pinks down the centre with lily-of-the-valley either side linked with bows of ribbon. It was fashionable, from the second decade of the eighteenth century until the end of the 1760s, for the stomacher to fill the opening in the front of a dress. It did not necessarily match the dress but was designed to harmonise with it and could be replaced by others, simpler or more elaborate. Small flowers, each about three inches high, are worked on the back of the bodice, on the sleeves, and on the overskirt. There are over two hundred flowers on the overskirt, each one different; although some of the species are the

Apron of black ribbed silk (detail). The flowers were worked with twisted silks of very fine thread in brilliant colours.

same, there will be a twist to a leaf or a twirl of a tendril that makes each individual. The richly embroidered hemline of the petticoat, encrusted with large flowers and leaves, has more flowers scattered above as if nonchalantly thrown, yet placed by her skilful hand in such a way as to be in perfect balance one with another. The flowers include winter jasmine, hawthorn berries, sweet pea, love-in-the-mist, lily-of-the-valley, forget-me-not, anemone, tulips, convolvulus, blue-bell, roses and many others, and are in long and short stitch. The skirt of the dress was not as exaggerated as those worn by very fashionable ladies, but this was typical of her sense of moderation:

I am glad you *detest* the tubs of hoops, – I keep within bounds, endeavouring to avoid all particularities of being *too much in* or *out* of fashion; youth and liveliness never prompted me to break through that rule, not considering I had graces enough of my own to carry off any extravagance, and now my years and station tie me down to that which has ever been my choice.

Inspiration for her needlework came to Mrs Delany when she travelled with the Dean. She likened the gentle golden yellows and browns in corn, cattle and bogs to those of the autumn, 'like a faded leaf in work.' Her embroidery of autumn leaves in worsted chenille was so close to nature it is thought she may have had them specially dyed to produce such subtlety. The importance of using the best thread was emphasised; flaxen thread was recommended for nankeen as cotton was considered insufficiently strong. So industrious was she with her needlework that Dr Delany remarked to a friend; 'She works even between the coolings of her tea.'

Many a happy hour was spent by the ladies of the neighbourhood helping each other with some of the larger items for their households; canvas carpets were often worked by a group. Mrs Delany was delighted to help and went out of her way to shop in Dublin for those of her friends in the Deanery of Down unable to get to good shops. But working a friend's carpet meant working her taste too; 'Monday, I went to Dublin, was two hours and a half choosing worsteds for a friend in the North, who is working a *fright* of a carpet!'

Of her own circle Mrs Delany was particularly fond of Mrs Forth Hamilton of Finglass, whose needlework equalled hers in delicacy. Mrs Hamilton's embroidery also used Mrs Delany's theme of plants for so many of her designs, to which she added butterflies, moths, dragon-flies, lady-birds, and even a small snail, sometimes

A design of fruit and flowers in a chinoiserie vase, drawn and pricked on paper as a pattern for decorating furnishings.

From this faded 19th-century photograph it is still possible to recognise the pinks and lily-of-the-valley which decorated the stomacher of Mrs Delany's court dress.

An English court dress embroidered in coloured silk and silver thread in an elaborate flower and shell design, 1745–50.

Drawings by Mrs Delany for her court dress.

A detail from the petticoat of the court dress, showing, among many others, her favourite flower, the lily-of-the-valley.

combining painting and needlework together in the same picture.
She often arrived at Delville by eight in the morning for breakfast in
the garden, before setting to work with her hostess at embroidery or
some other recreation. Mrs Vesey of Lucan, and Letitia Bushe were
close friends, too, and on one occasion, helped Mrs Delany in a
spring-cleaning chore: 'I set them all to work, gave each a dusting
cloth, brush, sponge and bowl of water, and set them to cleaning my
picture-frames. Bushe undertook cleaning the pictures, and egging
them out, whilst the carpenters and I fixed up the shelves for my
books and china; everybody that popped their head in, was *seized to
work*, no idler was admitted; a very merry working morning it was,
and my dressing-room is very spruce and handsome.' Another time
Mrs Delany helped Mrs Vesey who had 'a whim to have Indian
figures and flowers cut out and oiled, to be transparent, and pasted
on her dressing-room window in imitation of painting on glass, and
it has a very good effect; we go again next Friday to finish what we
began last week.'

With Mrs Delany's artistic talents widening to other mediums it was not surprising that she needed more room for her equipment and space to work. She wrote to her sister: 'I am going to make a very comfortable closet;–to have a dresser, and all manner of working tools, to keep all my stores for painting, carving, gilding, &c; for my own room is now so clean and pretty that I cannot suffer it to be strewed with litter, only books and work [needlework], and the closet belonging to it to be given up to prints, drawings, and my collection of fossils, petrifications, and minerals.'

Much as she enjoyed her different crafts Mrs Delany sometimes felt doubts about spending her time in this way. She wrote to her sister about the difference in their store-rooms:

Mine fits only an idle mind that wants amusement; yours serves either to supply your hospitable table, or gives cordial and healing medicines to the poor and sick. Your mind is ever turned to help, relieve, and bless your neighbours and acquaintance; whilst mine I fear (however I may sometimes flatter my self that I have a contrary disposition), is *too much filled* with amusements of no real estimation; and when people commend any of my performances I feel a consciousness that my time might have been better employed.

She was very much against the frittering away of time and opportunity, of which she saw so much in Society. She was only thirty-three when she wrote:

Nothing betrays so great an idleness of mind, as that *perpetual seeking out* of something to divert thought; and where people *have talents* for more rational entertainment than that of shuffling and dealing cards, it surprises and provokes me beyond all patience. I am not so great an enemy to cards as to be uneasy at them, but I would not make it my business to secure company *for that purpose*; when they come accidently in the way they are very well.

She was convinced that happiness came through building up one's own interests and to rely solely on outside diversions was not to lay the foundation for a happy old age. A decade later she observed:

Everybody is engaged in a more public way of diverting themselves, I have withdrawn myself from these sort of engagements, and find more pleasure in the quiet enjoyment of my own amusements at home than a crowd can give me; and it is very happy that as our season of life changes our taste for pleasures alter. In the spring and summer of life we *flutter and bask* in the sunshine of diversions–it is true we run the hazard of being tamed and seldom escape it; in the autumn and in the winter of life we by degrees seek for shade and shelter, and if we have made a good and prudent gathering of fruit and harvest, we may then have the full enjoyment of them, as long as the great Author and Giver thinks fit.

The happiness of Mrs Delany's life at this time was broken by the death of her sister. Anne died in July 1761 at Bristol where she was ordered by her doctor to the hot-wells where it was hoped that the waters might improve her failing health. Mary was particularly distressed, but she eased her grief by devoting herself to Anne's children. She became particularly fond of her niece Mary, to whom most of her letters were now addressed.

One pursuit which Mrs Delany enjoyed throughout her life was drawing and painting. She was keen that her niece should have drawing lessons as a child so it seems likely that she had herself enjoyed lessons while living with her aunt Lady Stanley. In 1731 William Hogarth offered to give her tuition, and as she admired his work it is likely that she accepted. She was certainly taught by Goupy and Lens. A book of hers in the National Gallery of Ireland, Dublin, shows about ninety-two sketches including some of the garden at Delville, scenes in the deanery, her brother's garden at Calwich and those of her friends. Another book containing ninety-three sketches was sold at auction in 1819 amongst Queen Charlotte's effects. Anything that caught her eye was recorded, sometimes hastily on a scrap of paper, as when she penned the Dean's corpulent figure on the back of an envelope.

Dr Delany, sketch by Mrs Delany in ink on the back of an envelope.

Portraits were a favourite subject; she painted all her immediate family and was lent paintings by friends to copy. She borrowed a painting from Archbishop Stone to reproduce: 'I have now dead-coloured all the figures (which are 4) of the Primate's Raphael, it is a charming picture, but will cost me many a groan before I finish.'

Whilst staying in Bath in 1760, Mrs Delany found herself studying a new fashion in portraits that brought, in her opinion, certain unacceptable innovations, for in the previous century a lady who was painted full length and with a musical instrument was considered definitely fast. There was a new artist who had settled in Bath who was creating a name for himself, and she was keen to see his work. 'This morning went with Lady Westmoreland to see Mr Gainsborough's picture ... There I saw Miss Ford's picture, a whole length with her guitar, a most extraordinary figure handsome and bold; but I should be very sorry to have anyone I loved set forth in such a manner.' For her own portrait attributed to Thomas Gainsborough she is depicted in a traditional position, seated half-profile and glancing towards the artist.

The painter and miniaturist Mr Barber lived in a house at the end of the Delanys' garden. Mrs Delany took an interest in his progress

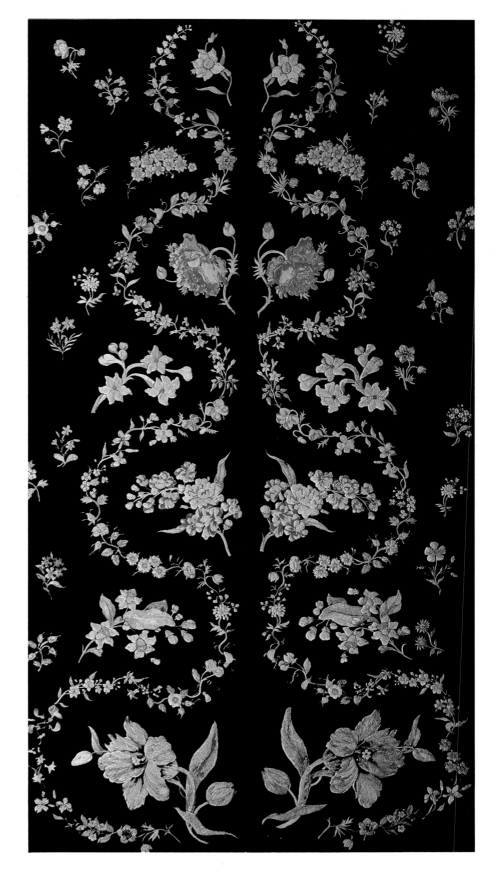

'Rococo-style' border of the overskirt to Mrs Delany's court dress.

LEFT A harebell, enlarged from the overskirt of Mrs Delany's court dress. About 3 inches high.

BELOW A poppy, embroidered by Mrs Delany on black silk.

BOTTOM Detail from the hem of the petticoat of Mrs Delany's court dress.

and was eager to help him become better known: 'Mr Barber has just finished another picture of me in enamel, which Mr Bristowe says, is better done than any he ever saw of Zincke's indeed I think it very finely enamelled; and I hope it will bring him into good business. Lord Massareen sits to him on Monday, and Mr Bristowe has promised to prevail, if possible, with Lord and Lady Chesterfield to sit to him, and that will bring him into fashion; he is very industrious and deserves to be encouraged.' This was another example of her practical help, for she knew that any struggling artist who was favoured by the Lord Lieutenant of Ireland and his wife was certain to have further orders. She expressed this sentiment in 1759: '. . . though I don't design to *exclude* myself from the Castle, I think it wrong to give up powerful acquaintance, even when they are not very valuable, they may be of some use some way to somebody or other.'

The amusement she had found in cutting paper when she was a

A painting in oils by Mrs Delany after Corregio, 1760. This was one of the many paintings lent to her by friends to copy.

child continued throughout her life. She cut and painted a set of miniature playing cards for Mary Dewes in 1752, about an inch long, and the following year cut an alphabet in card for her. Other examples of cut-work show three-dimensional pictures of birds cut in vellum; in one a cockatoo has wool placed between the bird and the background to give it shape, the feathers are cut almost as finely as actual feathers; a similar picture shows humming-birds drinking nectar from flowers, and another is a crested pheasant which stands sentinel on a tree stump.

At Longleat there are seven silhouettes believed to have been executed by Mrs Delany during her various visits. One of the silhouettes is painted black on white paper, but the remainder are executed in the following manner: each silhouette is cut in a sheet of white paper and this sheet is mounted on a black background, the black being visible through the silhouette holes in the white sheet.

The art of shell decoration reached a peak of popularity and elegance in the middle of the eighteenth century and Mrs Delany was one of its foremost practitioners. From decorating objects, she moved to the greater expanse of ceilings and walls, possibly inspired

ABOVE LEFT 'Broad Crested Cockatoo, native of New Holland', cut from one piece of vellum. The beak, eye, branch and leaves are painted. There are 56 individually cut feathers on the crest and neck alone. Overall measurement 6 × 7 inches.

ABOVE 'Fire-Backed Pheasant of Java'. An outstanding example of Mrs Delany's skill at cut-work. The bird is cut from one piece of vellum; the eyes, lower legs and tree stump are painted. Overall measurement 9 × 7 inches.

RIGHT A section of shell cornice from the Chapel at Delville, worked by Mrs Delany.

ABOVE A detail from the 'Fire-Backed Pheasant', showing the finely-cut tail feathers, with 86 cuts to an inch.

by the wish to imitate the perfection of the stucco work done by Dublin craftsmen at that time. The 'eating-parlour' at Delville had been decorated with cherubs' heads and tasselled ribbons, and a hook-nosed Roman emperor stared out from an oval of laurel leaves on the wall. In another room there were birds, swags of roses, vine leaves and grapes. In December 1750 she started work on the ceiling of Delville's chapel: 'Bushe reads alloud whilst I go on making shell flowers for the ceiling of the chapel. I have made 86 large flowers and about 30 small ones.' Later that month her enthusiasm is just as great: 'D.D. employs me every hour of the day for his chapel. I make the flowers and other ornaments by candle-light, and by daylight when I don't paint, put together the festoons that are for the ceiling.' Her bedroom, too, was decorated: 'My bow window has provoked me to a good deal of work . . . I am making festoons with shell-flowers in their *natural colours*, that are to go over the bow window . . . The coach is at the door, and we are going to Burdoyl, a strand about six miles off, in search of shells.'

Her active mind had been at work during the week, and further embellishments were added: 'I am making festoons with shell-flowers *chained-up* with silver bells, which will look very well on the crimson ground.' In the autumn she returned to the chapel: 'My chief works have been the ceiling of the chapel which I have formerly described, done with cards and *shells* in imitation of stucco. In the chancel are four Gothic arches . . . made *also of shells* in imitation of stucco, the arches no deeper than the thickness of the shells, to take off the plain look the walls would have without them. The wreath round the window is composed of oak-branches and vines made of cards; the grapes, nuts, and large periwinkles, the corn, *real wheat* painted, all to look like stucco.' George Montagu in a letter to Horace Walpole dated October 1761 wrote of Mrs Delany's work at Delville: 'All fitted up and painted by her own hand the stucco composed of shells and ears of corn the prettily-est disposed imaginable.' C.P. Curran in *Dublin Decorative Plasterwork of the 17th and 18th Century* writes of her shellwork: 'It was not a mere affair of arranging shells to an agreeable pattern. The various shells were coloured for different flowers and were set on edge disposed in concentric or natural forms, the petals achieving the effect of the finest stucco in high relief.' In England when visiting her cousin, Mrs Foley, at Stoke Edith near Hereford Mrs Delany made festoons of shells on the walls of a dressing-room which were likened to Grinling Gibbons' carving.

Because of the popularity of this pastime, travellers abroad returned with barrels filled with shells, bereaved families auctioned shell collections to raise money, and shells were to be found in shops, though they seem to have been very costly. Mrs Delany and her friend, the Duchess of Portland (who was also a collector and who had killed one thousand snails for their shells), called on Mr Deard, a jeweller in Pall Mall, to see 'a curious collection of shells. There were ten small drawers full – the number of shells inconsiderable; not to be called a collection as many shells were wanted but the shells were perfect of their kind, and some rare sorts, and so they had need for the price set on them is three hundred pounds!' Acquaintances offered to collect for her. One gave a tiled cockle too big to go in her cabinet, so it was placed on the floor underneath. 'It is as fine a shell as I ever saw – it is vulgarly called the Lion's Claw and comes from the West Indies.' At Bath her brother introduced to her 'a seafaring captain called Edwards who has promised me a box of shells from Guinea, Jamaica, &c.' She was careful to distinguish between the rare and common, referring to some as 'trumpery sorts, none that are fit for anything but common grotto work.' Mrs Delany was always on the look out for new rarities to add to her shell collection, but a visit to Mr Calcot, the philosopher, proved disappointing: 'his collection is rare and curious of spars, minerals and fossils, much as I have never seen and *un*answerable testimonies of the Deluge. But his heart is I believe of the petrified kind, and

Mrs Delany's hobby of shell-work involved trips along the coast to search for shells. This sketch is 'a view of y.ᵉ murrah of Wicklow', a beach some thirty miles south of Dublin.

encrusted with avarice, for he has *many* of *most sorts* in his collection, and he gave me not so much as a single grain of tin however I was not disappointed as I went for instruction and entertainment, though not without some *small hope* of a little gain.' She went on to see Mr Goldney's grotto, now in the grounds of Bristol University, 'the master of it is reckoned a great humorist and a niggard, but I was so fortunate as to take his fancy, and he gave me two or three pretty specimens of coral, and said I should have what I pleased.'

As her collection grew she became anxious to preserve it, particularly from the attentions of child visitors: 'Sir J. Meade is heir to a great estate, a child of six years old, most *unreasonably indulged* – a fine sensible boy, but under no *sort of command*, I had 20 frights for my

The Cottage, 'A sweeter spot on earth was never found'. This drawing, dated 1766, and the verses which accompany it, epitomise the ideal of rural bliss which Mary Delany sought and which, for twenty-five years, she found at Delville.

The Cottage

A sweeter spot on earth was never found.

MD: 1766

A sweeter spot of Earth was never found.

I look & look, & still with new delight;   To satisfy at once the smell, and Sight.
Such joy my Soul, such pleasure fills my Sight;   Nor sullen discontent; nor anxious care,
Here, the fresh Eglantine, exhales a breath;   Ev'n tho' brought hither, can inhabit here:
Whose odours are of power to raise from Death: But hence they flee, as from their mortal Foe;
And Nature seems to vary the delight,   For this sweet place, can only pleasure know.

china, shells and books, his little fingers seized everything with such impetuosity that I was ready to box him; had I been his mama I should have been *most heartily ashamed of him*.' When the Delanys were away from Delville for the summer and lent their house to friends who also had a young son, she took some precautions: 'I hope the boy won't break and rifle my shell cabinet! I have taken the liberty to order it to be constantly covered.'

This idyllic life at Delville was not without its clouds; in 1750 Mrs Delany wrote of the Dean's spirits being 'much turmoiled with his Tennison lawsuit.' Aspersions had been made by his first wife's relatives that he had burnt a paper with intent to defraud them of money. Undoubtedly he had been careless, and the lawsuit was lost; costs were high, and they had to adjust to a lower income. It was, however, necessary to pursue the action to clear the Dean's name of 'spoliation'. After spending many months in London, with the case finally taken to the House of Lords, Mrs Delany wrote in March 1758:

'A cause never was so *well attended*, nor a more *universal joy seen* than when Lord Mansfield, after an hour and a half's speaking with angelic oratory, pronounced the decree in our favour; the 'spoliation' *entirely thrown aside* . . . The decree that now takes place makes D.D. liable to pay 3000 pounds . . . but the grand point is gained, and his enemies, if they have any modesty, must be greatly abashed . . . I am going now my rounds of visits to those whose husbands attended.'

The anxiety of the court case took its toll on Dr Delany's health and in 1754 he had an attack of the palsy. He recovered to enjoy another twelve years at Delville but died in May 1768, aged eighty-three. For Mrs Delany it was the end of an era of happiness, best summed up by her description of the summer of 1750: 'D.D. up to his chin haymaking on the lawn under my closet and the whole house fragrant with the smell of it . . . the garden is Paradaisical.'

6 *A Widow Again*

Mary Dewes, Mrs Delany's niece.

In her sixty-ninth year Mrs Delany faced bereavement with characteristic fortitude. She knew she had much to be thankful for in the devotion of her relatives and friends, in particular her niece Mary Dewes, whose development to maturity was guided by her aunt with tender affection. Mary was encouraged in her artistic pursuits, but there are warnings too throughout her aunt's letters:

You cannot have too many *innocent* amusements, provided you do *not neglect* what is essential to learn; and indeed an ingenious mind will always find most entertainment for those employments that improve it . . . if it turns to more frivolous curiosity it will lead you astray, and instead of finding you are in the midst of roses and every desirable fruit and flower, you will be entangled in briars and nettles, and all sorts of noxious weeds. Our business in this world is for preparing for another, and in order to make that exchange a happy one we must act up to the name we have taken upon us of Christianity . . . The rules are plain and easy, if indolence or luxury do not interfere and blind us. And a habit of doing our duty regularly is the best guard against the evils and temptations that beset us, and by accustoming ourselves to that regularity we shall find no manner of difficulty, but rather be uneasy at any omission.

When J.J. Rousseau, the French philosopher, took a house at Wootton near her brother at Calwich, Mrs Delany became alarmed that his philosophy might influence Mary who often stayed with her uncle.

Now for a word about Monsieur Rousseau, who has gained so much of your admiration. His writings are ingenious, no doubt, and were they weeded from the false and erroneous sentiments that are blended through his works (as I have been told), they would be as valuable as they are entertaining.

It was through her visits to Calwich that Mary Dewes met John Port of Ilam, and after enquiries were made of his suitability as a husband, and in spite of opposition from Bernard Granville, she was married at Bulstrode with the blessing of Mrs Delany and the Dowager Duchess of Portland, and settled at Ilam, a few miles away from her uncle.

After the death of her husband Mrs Delany was invited by the Dowager Duchess of Portland to make a long visit to the Duchess's home of Bulstrode, near Gerrards Cross, Buckinghamshire. The Duchess was the daughter of the second Earl of Oxford and the widow of the second Duke of Portland. She was fourteen years younger than Mrs Delany but their shared artistic and intellectual interests had made them very close friends. They had kept in touch throughout Mrs Delany's years in Ireland and met each year during her visits to England. Now that they were both widowed their friendship grew even closer, and Mrs Delany stayed at Bulstrode for six months of each year, generally from spring to autumn, for the next seventeen years.

It was a stimulating household, for the Duchess's lively intellect and generous hospitality attracted many people of renown to Bulstrode. Politicians, explorers, botanists, gardeners, artists, actors, men of letters, church dignitaries and members of the royal family all came to visit her. The Duchess had a magpie's enthusiasm for collecting, made 'improvements' to her garden, and kept a menagerie of unusual birds and animals, but her chief interest was botany. In the autumn of 1768 Mrs Delany wrote:

Mr Ehret is very busy for the Dss of Portland, he has already painted above a hundred and fifty English plants, and now they are collected together their beauty is beyond what we have a notion of.

George Dionysius Ehret has been judged by some to have been the finest botanical artist of all time. He was the son of a market gardener at Heidelberg and trained as a gardener, but at twenty-two he took up botanical draughtsmanship, and arrived in England in 1735. The Duchess was one of his chief patrons and paid him two guineas each for his water colours on vellum, besides engaging him to teach her daughters to paint. His visits to Bulstrode must have been greatly enjoyed by the two ladies, for their botanical knowledge was considerable, guided by the family chaplain the Rev. John Lightfoot, one of the most distinguished botanists of that century. In the autumn of 1769 Ehret returned to Bulstrode: 'Mr Ehret is here' wrote Mrs Delany to her niece,

. . . and the Dss is very busy adding to her English herbal; she has been

Ilam in Dovedale, where John and Mary Port lived. Mrs Delany often visited the Ports at Ilam and took special delight in their growing family.

RIGHT 'Azalea Viscosa' [*Rhododendron viscosum*]

•

OVERLEAF
LEFT 'Rosa Spinosissima, Burnet Rose' [*Rosa pimpinellifolia*]. There are 65 thorns, cut in one piece with the stem; RIGHT 'Rosa, Cluster Damask', showing an insect bite cut in a leaf.

'Cynoglossum Omphalodes, Hounds tongue', now known as Cynoglossum Verna. There is a real leaf on the right. This was one of the few blue-flowered plants Mrs Delany copied.

'Asclepias Curasavica, Swallow wort'. The plant was given to Mrs Delany by James Lee. She was in her 80th year.

transported at the discovery of a *new wild plant*, a Helleboria . . . Mr Lightfoot has deserted us. *The briars* of the *law* have laid hold of him when he would much rather pursue the *briars of the hedges*! But next week we hope will restore our botanical master; en attendant we have Mr Ehret, who goes out in search of curiosities in the fungus way, as this is now their season, and reads us a lecture on them an hour before tea, whilst her Grace examines all the celebrated authors to find out their classes. This is productive of much learning and of excellent observations from Mr Ehret, uttered in *such a dialect* as sometimes puzzles me (though he calls it English) to find out what foreign language it is.

Ehret had married Susannah Kennet, the sister-in-law of Philip Miller, who became one of the great botanical horticulturalists of the eighteenth century. Miller was appointed by Sir Hans Sloane to be in charge of the Chelsea Physic Garden in 1722 with the title of Gardener, developing Chelsea into the finest botanical garden in the world. He too had stayed at Bulstrode in December 1753 when Mrs Delany was visiting there from Ireland. She wrote: 'Who do you think is here? why no less a person than Mr Miller . . . he is now in the library up to his elbows in books of prints.' She was there when he made a return visit:

We have had the great Mr Miller, of Chelsea, here for some days; you may think how busy the botanists were, but he is a great politician and would rather talk of state affairs. He is a well-behaved man, but does not seem to want a good opinion of himself; people that really have merit and have been useful to the world, may be forgiven the foible of vanity, though those who *bear their faculties meekly* are more truly valuable.

Margaret Cavendish Harley, wife of the second Duke of Portland, from an enamel by Zincke.

Philip Miller's *Gardener's Dictionary* became a classic and was sought by all keen horticulturalists here and abroad. His *Gardening Kalendar*, too, was in demand; 'Directing what works are necessary to be done every month, in the kitchen, fruit and pleasure gardens and in the conservatory, with an account of the particular seasons for the propagation and use of all sorts of . . . plants and trees etc.' This useful guide was followed by Mrs Delany throughout the seasons in Ireland.

The garden at Bulstrode was to receive the same rapturous praise and to give as much enjoyment to Mrs Delany as her beloved Delville. She continued her habit of rising early and walked for an hour or so before breakfast, sometimes taking a basket of food to feed the animals in the park, and the peacocks and guinea fowl in the garden, and drawing them in her sketchbook. It was a peaceful time of the day which she treasured:

'Fort St Davids Bull', drawn by Mrs Delany in Bulstrode Park. In 1753 Mrs Delany wrote enthusiastically of this bull: 'it is tame as a lamb and had a very good-humoured countenance: his horns were broken off in a duel with an animal of his own kind.'

Surely an application to natural beauties must enlarge the mind? Can we view the wonderful texture of every leaf and flower, the dazzling and varied plumage of birds, the glowing colours of flies &c., &c., and their infinite variety, without saying, *'wonderful and marvellous art thou in all thy works!'* And this house, with all belonging to it, is a *noble school* for contemplations!

Mrs Delany had remarkably good health, no doubt helped by her liking for fresh air, and her creative outlook on life, and she wrote of her frustration when, in 1776, 'a little accident by the bite of a venemous fly on my ancle, just above the shoe, has made me a prisoner for a fortnight past, and very cautious of walking'. But she later reported: 'I have walked for an hour in the garden, read an account of the Fete Champetre in the newspaper, puzzled my head with 10 pages of philosophy, ate my breakfast, and now am going to settle to work.'

Mrs Delany and the Duchess spent many mornings, if fine, driving through the park in a chaise in search of botanical specimens. So enticing was Bulstrode in the summer months that Mrs Delany regretted any intrusion into this idyllic scene, and jokingly wished the Duchess's daughters would issue their invitations to their mother later in the year: 'Bulstrode and its millions of charms, in the midst of haymaking, botanizing, *roses*, and Mr Lightfoot *too*. I wish these ladies would consider all these things, and not make demands on the Duchess of Portland till the dreary months of November, December and January!'

A grotto was designed and ornamented with shells by Mrs Delany at Bulstrode, using material sent by relatives in Cornwall and Derbyshire, but not without misunderstanding between her and the gardener who did much of the labouring: 'I am just returned from 3 hours attendance on Mr Davies, who is an excellent taskmaster for

'A view of Bulstrode Park', drawn by Mrs Delany.

the exercise of patience and is duller than the rocks he hammers up.' A watchful eye was kept on the progress of the grotto for the next two months, 'All the difficult part is finished, and now no blunder can take place in our absence!' It would be equally entertaining to know Mr Davies's thoughts of his directress. As the project neared completion she wrote, 'The cave goes on briskly, and now draws near a conclusion my zeal to get it finished increases, whilst I am working away heaving rude stones together, I am entertained by the blackbird that feeds its young in the opening of the top, and picks up the crumbs that I strewed on the window for him, giving me a little twitter of thanks.'

But life at Bulstrode was not without its irritations; the Duchess was involved in a dispute with local people who wished to build a public highway through Bulstrode Park. Such a prospect appalled Mrs Delany, who, as ever championing the Duchess's cause, exclaimed: 'It wd be vexatious to have her fine verdure at the mercy of wheels and scampering hordes and all her *happy creatures* disturbed in their quiet possessions. Her great civility to her neighbours is *ill requitted*, but a gentleman (belonging to the law) said here the other day what is very true, that "the law abominates all civility".'

In 1771 two eminent botanists stayed at Bulstrode: Joseph Banks (1743–1820) and Daniel Solander (1733–82). Banks, with Solander as his assistant, had recently returned from his journey round the world, having accompanied Captain Cook on his voyage of discovery in the *Endeavour*. Fascinating tales were recounted to the ladies at the dinner table of the travels, for Captain Cook had two missions to complete when he sailed from Plymouth on 25 August 1768. First, he was to observe the transit of Venus for the Royal Society as the British part in an international scientific effort, which had for its object the determination of the earth's distance from the sun, and second, he was to carry on the process of geographical discovery set in motion by the Admiralty with Admiral J. Byron's voyage of 1764–6. Banks's particular interest on this voyage was finding plants that would be of economic benefit if introduced into other countries. His herbarium was one of the most important in existence and is now in the Natural History Museum, as is also his library. The plants brought on board for careful study, and the seeds stored for bringing back to this country, were gathered in such profusion by Solander in one area that Captain Cook named it Botany Bay.

Banks, who had inherited a fortune on the death of his father, gave Mrs Delany and the Duchess an indication of their plans for publishing the botanical discoveries. 'They are preparing an account of their voyage; but the Natural History will be a work by itself, entirely at the expense of Mr Banks for which he laid by ten thousand pounds,' wrote Mrs Delany excitedly, 'he has already the drawings of everything (birds, beasts, plants and views) that were remarkable; the work to be set in order, that is the history written, by Mr Hawksworth, under the inspection of Mr Banks and Dr Solander; it will hardly come out in my time, as it will consist of at least fourteen volumes in folio. As this was *private* talk perhaps it should not be mentioned in general.' The two explorers were fortunate to have two good listeners who could also appreciate all their botanical observations.

Banks's house in London was for many years a centre for the meeting of scientists and the exchange of ideas, so Mrs Delany and the Duchess were particularly delighted to accept an invitation from him a few weeks after his visit to Bulstrode:

We were yesterday at Mr Banks to see some of the fruits of his travels, and were delighted with paintings of the Otaheitie plants, quite different from anything the Dss *ever* saw, so they must be very new to me! They have

Mrs Delany was fascinated by the specimens of strange and exotic plants brought back from Captain Cook's South Pacific voyage. This dried specimen of *Banksia* was collected from Botany Bay.

A silhouette cut by Mrs Delany in the late 1760s, showing the children of the third Viscount Weymouth and his wife Elizabeth, daughter of the Duchess of Portland. Boards were secured to the children's shoulder to improve posture.

brought the seeds of some of them which they think will do here; several of them are blossoms of *trees* as big as the largest *oak*, and so covered with flowers that their beauty can hardly be imagined; there is one in particular (the name I cannot recollect) that bears vast flowers, larger and somewhat of the appearance of the largest poppy when full blown, the leaves all fungid; the petals that are like threads, are at the calyx *white*, by degrees shaded with pale purple, and ending with *crimson*.

This description shows the botanist and the artist in Mrs Delany, which was to serve her so well when she began the following year to create her flower pictures in coloured cut paper.

Under the knowledgeable Lightfoot, minerals of all sorts were studied too:

I cannot tell you how busy we have been in examining the varieties of stalactities, selenites, ludus helmontii, &.&. Much learning I have heard, some of which I hope I have retained.

Their studies were undertaken with the seriousness of professionals, and when her niece Mary sent a box of coal and shells from Derbyshire she was told:

. . . you must inform us of their birth and parentage, particularly of some brown moss-like substance that was pack'd into the largest cockle, and a little brassish, copperish, goldish thread-like stuff adhering to a bit of slate or coal, and which has puzzled even Mr Lightfoot to find out without you inform us where they were found, whether on rock or tree, or bog? you must be very minute in your account; nothing less can satisfye such accurate enquirers.

With their 'comfortable litters' around them in the drawing-room the two ladies worked at their various hobbies. Mrs Delany needed a good-sized table-top to continue her cut paper designs.

She made an album of silhouettes depicting Mary Port's children including one of herself nursing Mary's eldest daughter Georgina; she designed and cut paper to cover chimney boards which screened the empty grates in the summer, and plenty of space must have been needed for her flower collages, described in detail in the next chapter. But one of the joys of a large house was room for every pastime:

Mr Lightfoot and botany go on as usual; we are now in the chapter of Agarick's and Boletus's &., &., this being the time of their perfection and her Grace's breakfast room, which is now the repository of sieves pans, platters, and filled with all the productions of *that nature*, are spread on tables, windows, chairs, which with books of all kinds (opened in their useful places), make an agreeable confusion; sometimes notwithstanding twelve chairs and a couch, *it is* indeed a little *difficult* to find a seat!

But there were occasions when these pastimes had to be cleared up:

A gracious visit from her R.H. Princess Amelia [second daughter of George II] has made some little disturbance even in this place. All the comfortable sophas and great chairs, all the piramids of books (adorning *almost every chair*), all the tables and *even the spinning wheel* were banish'd for that day, and the blew damask chairs set in prim form around the room, only one arm'd chair placed in the middle for her Royal Highness; she came in a post coach and four, only attended by two footmen and a groom. She was met at the perimeter of the park by the keeper, who took her (not the common way), but thro' the bosom . . . – a three mile cut which the Duchess had landscaped in her park. After dinner the princess was shown round the house when she saw 'all my frippery works, all of which she graciously commended' and returned to Gunnersbury by moonlight.

As Mrs Delany and the Duchess enjoyed company and good conversation, they paid many calls. On one occasion they drove in a chaise to visit the eccentric Richard Bateman, who was altering his house to make it look like a monastery.

Last Thursday we went to Old Windsor to see Mr Bateman's, which I had not seen since his converting it from Indian to Gothic. Its outward appearance is venerable – arched porticos and windows, Gothic towers and battlements, encompassed and shaded with large trees, the verdure fine, the river winding most beautifully . . . the walls are embossed with indescribable oddities brought from all corners of the world; . . . his library is indeed as *fribblish* as himself, and so furnished with looking-glasses that had it the property of representing to him his inside as well as outside, it might read him better lesson than he could find in his whole collection of books, and show him his own insignificancy. You'll say I am satirical, I don't mean to be so, but I was a little provoked by his chapel which is within his dressing-room . . . it is an exact representation of a popish chapel

Mr and Mrs Garrick taking tea
on the lawn of their Thameside
house. Zoffany, 1760.

expensively decorated . . . and a thousand things relating to ceremonies
that I don't understand . . . what must offend every serious observer must
be the intent of this chapel, for if he does *not* make use of it in *good earnest* his
making a joke of it is *shocking*.

The visit made a considerable impression on the ladies, for, when
passing his house a few weeks later, Mrs Delany wrote that they
'moralised on the vanities of human life'.

An invitation that was particularly enjoyed was to David
Garrick's house beside the Thames. Mr and Mrs Garrick were
much admired by them not only for his superb acting, but for their
pleasing manners. The Garricks had been invited to stay at
Bulstrode in 1769 shortly after the Jubilee celebrations at Stratford-
on-Avon in commemoration of Shakespeare, and the following
summer Mrs Delany and the Duchess were entertained by them at
their house beside the Thames:

Mr Garrick did the honours of his house *very respectfully*, and tho' in high spirits seemed sensible of the honour done them . . . Nobody else there but Lady Weymouth, the Dss's eldest daughter, and Mr Bateman. As to Mrs Garrick, the more one sees her the better one must like her; she seems *never* to depart from a perfect propriety of behaviour, accompanied with good sense and gentleness of manners, and I cannot help looking on her as a *wonderful creature*, considering all circumstances relating to her. The house is singular (which you know I like), and seems to owe its prettiness and elegance to her good taste.

After an excellent dinner they passed into the garden much admired in design for its shade and shelter too:

Shakespeare's Temple at the end of the improvement, where we drank tea and coffee, and where there is a very fine statue of Shakespeare in white marble, and a great chair with a large carved frame, that was *Shakespeare's own chair* . . . Many were the relics we saw of the favourite poet.

It is interesting to read Lady Llanover's note appended to this letter, where she gives the view of a Victorian on the status of the Garricks. She wrote:

These few words are a high testimony to Garrick's tact and good breeding, as few persons, in his class of life, know how to be 'respectful' and yet in 'high spirits', which is the greatest test of real refinement.

Travel in the eighteenth century was no respecter of persons, whether the journey was long or short, and Mrs Delany had many adventures. When she travelled from Bulstrode to Whitehall where the Duchess lived in the winter, she wrote:

The chief postillion and his horse tumbled down, and we were obliged to get out of the chaise in the middle of the road; at first the shock was very great – as we had reason to think the man must be very much hurt if not

The Coach Overturned, a print of 1770.

The sedan chair of Sir John Dolben (1684–1716). With its painted leather panels, copper mounts and nail decoration, and brocade lining, the manufacture of this chair combined the skill of the cabinet-maker, upholsterer, metal-worker and painter.

LEFT 'Celsia Arcturus, Bastard Mullein', a gift from Mr Yalden. There is a real leaf in the centre.

killed; but, providentially, he was neither, only his leg a little bruised; but it was a frightful sight, and we neither recovered it for the day.

But another servant was less fortunate:

The newspapers, I suppose, informed you of the unhappy end of one of the Duchess of Portland's maids, who was thrown out of the waggon; the wheels ran over her, and she lived three hours in exquisite misery: this melancholy accident damped all our spirits extremely.

Accidents such as these were due to the bad state of the roads; it was a common occurrence for coaches to overturn. It took George II and Queen Caroline the whole night to travel from Kew to St James, when their coach turned over. Lady Carteret travelling with both her daughters pregnant suffered the same frightening experience. The Young Pretender's rising in 1745 showed that improved roads were necessary for the defence of the country, and 450 Acts were passed between 1760 and 1774 for the construction and upkeep of highways. Just how rough the roads were is indicated in expressions by Mrs Delany such as, 'had no occasion to get out of the coach the whole way' or, 'No accident or fright all the way'.

Highwaymen were a very real threat; the third Duke of Portland was robbed of his purse containing twenty guineas and his watch at Putney, and Mrs Delany described another attack in a letter to her brother:

Lord Berkeley one day last week, coming from London in his post chaise between 5 and 6 o'clock ten miles this side of London was attacked by a highwayman. As soon as he came to the chaise door Lord Berkeley shot at him with a blunderbuss. He rode off, and the footman behind the chaise fired another pistol at the man, which made him reel and drop off his horse and he expired in a few minutes.

For short distances sedan chairs were used, though these were not always easy to come by, especially in the summer when the chairmen were harvesting or hop-picking. But there were hazards even in the slow-moving sedans; the Duchess of Beaufort's chairmen bounced her against Mrs Delany's door and broke one of the glasses of the chair; Mrs Delany sent a lamenting card the next day: 'I did not know it till she was gone, and it really vexed me.' The same indignity happened to Mrs Delany when calling on Lady Westmoreland:

Coming out from the house, as soon as I got into my chair, the chairmen fairly overturned it, *fairly* I may say, for not a glass was broken nor was I the least hurt; I own I was a little terrified, and Lord Westmoreland hearing the bustle at the door, *found me topsy turvy*. He insisted on my getting out of my chair, which I did, drank a glass of water, sat half an hour in his library.

The chairs of the wealthy were often fitted out magnificently: 'Lady Dunkerron's sedan is yellow velvet, embroidered and imbossed with silver,' wrote Mrs Delany, whose eye missed none of the detail. The Duchess of Marlborough's chair was stolen for its cushions of crimson velvet, while she was in chapel, and Lady Frances Ludlow's chair was most exotic, in the form of an Indian house.

From the middle to the end of the eighteenth century there was political unrest in Europe, North America, and at home. In the 1750s a struggle was going on for possession of North America between Great Britain and France. As the families of her friends were involved in the fighting Mrs Delany became very concerned: 'Lord Fitzmaurice is going full of martial fire to America and my poor friend Mrs Hamilton's 4th son on the same expedition; youth and bravery make that admirable to them – I hope their ardour will be crowned with success, and I am glad to see a spark of bravery left.' In 1774 she and her friends were alarmed by the unrest in America: 'The American affairs are now the only topick of conversation'. The Parliamentary scene was watch'd ruefully by Mrs Delany as the Tories and Whigs argued their policies. 'As for policticks they are as they have been for months. Those *out* railing at those *in*, and those *in* too well fortified by the advantages of their situation to mind their railing!'

The House of Lords was shocked in April 1778 when Lord Chatham [Pitt] collapsed on the floor when rising to answer a question on America. Mrs Delany wrote:

Yesterday died Lord Chatham; he never recovered his fall in the House of Lords, but I daresay it was a consolation to him, under all his sufferings, to think that he died in his calling. Many panegyricks, many aspersions, will be banded backwards and forwards as *no man* ever was *so high or lower* in his sentiments, and in the estimation of the world; but he *had* undoubtedly great abilities, and *he had* served his country. He would have been a truly great character, had not an unbounded *ambition*, and a *vanity* hardly to be equalled, tarnished his good qualities. What havock do those 2 great underminers of virtue make in the human heart!

In London the Gordon Riots caused an orgy of destruction which lasted a week, and full order was not restored for another three days; almost five hundred people were killed or wounded. After a mild measure in Parliament to ease the restrictions on Catholics, the half-mad Lord George Gordon assembled a mob in June 1780, and with the old cry of 'No Popery', marched them towards the House of Commons to demand repeal. The rabble got out of control, pillaged

Catholic chapels, broke open prisons, and set fire to a distillery, proceeding to get drunk. Mrs Delany living in St James's Place was defenceless. The Duchess of Portland persuaded her to leave her house and spend a night with her at Privy Garden, Whitehall, before travelling the next day to Bulstrode. 'Some houses in St James's Place and Street were *threatened*', she wrote to Mary Port:

> . . . and here at Whitehall I have begun my letter, and can assure you, tho' I got very little sleep, I am this morning surprisingly well, notwithstanding many shocking agitations, which the universal distress must occasion . . . Lord Bute (and Lady Bute) are gone out of town; but I fear there will be as *little mercy* shown to *his* house as to *Lord Mansfield's* in Bloomsbury Square. Thank God *he* and his family are safe and well, but *his house* with everything in it is *burnt to the ground*! and Kenwood (Ld Mansfield's country house) would have met the same fate had not the militia saved it yesterday.

When in London, where Mrs Delany generally spent the winter months, she entertained friends and enjoyed the opportunity to view places of interest. In 1774 she went to Greek Street in Soho: 'I am just returned from viewing the Wedgwood-ware that is to be sent to the Empress of Russia. It consists I believe of as many pieces as there are days in the year, if not hours ... I feel quite giddy at looking at so much crockery ware.' Another call was to Christie's sale-room close by to see the Van Dyck painting, *Madonna and Child*, which was expected to sell for £4000; she also visited Sir Joshua Reynolds' house to see the portraits he was painting.

As Mrs Delany was musical and played the harpsichord well, she was glad of an excuse to accept invitations to the many concerts that were held in private houses, especially as it meant a chance to see what the fashionable guests were wearing. Even in her

seventies she thrived on these evening entertainments, and slept all the better for them. Fashions were becoming extreme both for their narrow waists and high hairstyles which would be made even higher by ornaments of feathers and other adornments. In May 1780 she reported:

Last night I was at Mrs Walsingham's concert on her opening her new house . . . The concert was splendid; rows above rows of fine ladies *towering tops* . . . I must own I could not help considering them with some astonishment, and lamenting that so absurd, inconvenient, and unbecoming a fashion should last so long, for though every year has produced some alteration, the *enormity* continues, and one of the most beautiful ornaments of nature, fine hair, is entirely disguised; . . . this is a subject as delicate to treat of as politics, so I don't venture at it in conversation, but give vent here by way of digression . . . I had a comfortable seat on a sofa by her Grace and Lady Bute, and *we* were the only flat caps in the room.

The following winter the fashions were as extreme as ever, and she thought it prudent to warn her niece of the dangers of these fashionable eccentricities:

ABOVE LEFT A satirical print ridicules the fashion for exaggeratedly high hairstyles.

ABOVE Mrs Delany was not alone in criticising the absurdity of the fashion for tight lacing, as a print of 1770 shows.

I hope Miss Sparrow will not fall into the absurd fashion of ye *wasp-waisted* ladies. Dr Pringle declares he has had four of his patients *martyrs* to that folly (indeed wickedness), and when they were opened it was evident that their *death* were occasioned by *strait lacing*.

But Mary Port may well have been secretly delighted at the smart cap that she had asked her aunt to buy for her, and of which Mrs Delany wrote: 'The cap I sent (tho' fashionable) I thought *enormous*, but could not wait for another and was assured ye might squeeze and *bend* the wires to ye taste.' The cap, together with 'Ceville oranges and jar of raissins bought of Koffin in the Haymarket', were sent by carrier to Ashbourne, the nearest town to the Ports' home.

Sometimes Mrs Delany joined the Blue Stockings at Mrs Montagu's house in Hill Street, but, though she was included in their circle, she never wished to be a frequent visitor in such an intellectual group: 'I went by invitation to Mrs M., the *witty* and *the lean* and found a formidable circle! I had a *whisper* with Mrs Boscawen, another with Lady Bute, and a *wink* from the Dss of Portland – *poor diet* for one who loves a plentiful meal of social friendship.' It was the more informal gatherings of social discourse that appealed to her, and an account of a few days in February when Mrs Delany was nearly eighty gives an insight into how much she enjoyed meeting people, and how popular she was: 'At twelve came Dr Cole with his friend Mrs Symonds, and afterwards Mr Martheille, Lady Andover, and Miss F. and Lady Stamford, who came from Whitehall to *spirit me up* to accept Lord Exeter's ticket for his concert.' The morning closed with visits by Court Dewes, her nephew, and Mr Smelt; and:

the evening circle was Lady Bute, Mrs Vesey and Miss Gregory, Lady Beaulieu, Lord Dartmouth, Lady Stamford, Duchess of Portland till eleven . . . yesterday morning I had only Mr Montagu, Mr Mulso, Mrs Boscawen, Miss Jennings, and at seven came her Grace's coach to convey me to Lady Stamford's and together we went, and I must own I had not reason to repent of my undertaking; it was neither hot nor crowded. The musical band choice . . . slept better than for many nights before.

As she became older she spent more time at home, though still enjoying the company of her callers, who talked over the topics of the day. 'My little circle last night discussed the trial of the Dss of Kingston', she wrote in April 1776. Elizabeth Chudleigh had secretly married Augustus John Hervey, later third Earl of Bristol. They had soon tired of each other, and Elizabeth obtaining a separation from him was declared spinster by court. She became the mistress of the Duke of Kingston, whom she 'married' in 1768 and whose wealth she inherited on his death in 1773, but she was accused of bigamy by the Duke's nephew three years later and declared guilty by the House of Lords. To Mrs Delany, who believed that those of high rank should set an example of good behaviour, such fraudulent conduct as masquerading in a rank to which one had no real entitlement was shocking:

She has her state coach following her wherever she bestows her presence, with three or four *ladies* (or rather *misses*) called her maids of honour. She wears a sack sometimes white sometimes other colours, trimmed with roses of ribbon, in each a large diamond, no cap, and diamonds in her hair, and some gee-gaws hovering over her head; a tucker edged with diamonds, a little twist with a jewel dangling, and no more of a tippet than serves to make her fair bosom conspicuous rather than to hide it.

When the Duke died, society waited inquisitively to hear the will, Mrs Delany amongst them: 'Everybody gapeing for the Duke of Kingston's will – £4000 a year he settled on her at his *marriage* (if *such* it may be allow'd)'. So many people wanted to attend the trial that it was by ticket only: 'All the world, great and small, are gone to Westminster Hall'. Mrs Delany was amused by 'the solicitude for tickets, the distress of rising early to be time enough for a place, the anxiety about hairdressers (poor souls hurried out of their lives), mortification that feathers and flying lappets should be laid aside for that day as they would obstruct the view from those who sat behind.'

There was much discussion when Lord Chesterfield's letters to his son were published in 1774, a year after his death. Mrs Delany had known him and his wife when he was Lord Lieutenant in Ireland, and she had some pointed remarks to make after she had read the letters:

All the world are now reading Lord Chesterfield's letters; I have begun them, they are a *medley* of *sense*, *knowledge of the world*, attention to the minutest article of good breeding, *entertainments*, *satire*, *and immorality*, and *not* a few *inconsistencys*; for at the same time he recommends decency of behaviour and avoiding all low vices, he recommended *everything* that *can shake* the foundation of virtue and religion, tho' at times he mentions *both* as necessary . . . The conclusion of his life showed how inferior his heart was to his head: unkind and ungrateful to an *excellent wife*.

Mrs Delany's deeply felt resentment at the injustice so often meted out to women is voiced when she learnt that the heir, a distant relative, had been left near twenty thousand pounds a year, but Lady Chesterfield had been left only four thousand a year, which was chiefly her own money:

It was hard, considering how good a wife she had been, and what a good fortune she was to him, *not* to leave her in *very* affluent circumstances for her own life. *He* even *left away* her jewels, which were *chiefly* purchased with her *own money*, but *the law* restored them to her as her own paraphanalia . . . So vanity, as you say, had taken possession of him, and drove out all gratitude and natural affection; and such is the case with human frailty if not well guarded against. Prejudice and passion are powerful enemies to struggle with if once indulged.

Although Mrs Delany's income was much smaller than that of most of her friends she was almost totally free of the day-to-day household activities of cooking and cleaning that most women in the late twentieth century have to attend to. She had a butler George, who went with her to Bulstrode, a cook, and Smith, who was her housekeeper for thirty-five years, and for the period she was in Ireland she had engaged a woman to wash her laces. There was the occasional annoyance with staff, but she never dismissed any of them lightly, and was careful to help find employment for any servants amongst her friends. Molly Butcher, her maid, who had been with her for several years, was proving rather a trial at St James's Place, but Mrs Delany thought that marriage, which was one of the chief reasons for leaving service, was unlikely to solve this problem: 'She has tired me out with her temper. But alas she has no outward charms to attract tho' *she thinks* the shoemaker that attends her is *not* insensible. I doubt it false fire.' Friends and relatives in the country supplied her with food for her larder, venison, turkey, chicken and hares, a Périgord pie, and potted rabbits once all arrived within one week.

Mary Port, who led an unsophisticated life at Ilam with a growing family to attend to, was not only kept informed of the social news from London, but sought the advice of her aunt on domestic matters. Mrs Delany encouraged her to be firm with her children, just as she had encouraged Mary's mother to be strict with hers:

Early wrong indulgencies are hardly ever rooted out . . . but nothing is easier (if soon eno' begun) than making a child obedient and humble; nothing so unsurmountable as obstinacy and pride when suffered to grow with them; it so totally corrupts the heart and perverts the understanding so that they grow insensible to the impressions of tenderness or gratitude.

The loneliness of women in Mary Port's social position, living in comparative isolation in the Derbyshire Peak district, long before the development of village community life as we know it today where intellectual and social needs are to a certain extent catered for, is made poignant by her letters written in 1784 to Mrs Anne Viney, a faithful friend in Gloucester. In the summer she wrote:

My last little girl Fanny, who is just turned a year old is a dear little *Fair, Fat, good humoured* Cherubim and I trust in God she will be the *last*, I have no reason to think to the contrary at present – Mr Port has had a flying gout for which he has gone to spend a fortnight at Buxton.

Mary's brothers reported further ill health, coughs and sore throats in the autumn, which without the advantage of twentieth-century medicine and warmer houses were a constant trial in the colder months. In December John Port wrote to Mrs Viney of his wife's 'nervous complaint and [she is] forbidden to write for 7 months', which must surely have increased her sense of isolation and depression.

The famous Portland Vase, the antique glass vase bought by the Duchess of Portland from Sir William Hamilton.

Much of the information of Mrs Delany's life when she was eighty-three years old is supplied from the diary of Miss Mary Hamilton, who had a position at court to Queen Charlotte. Mary Hamilton had a zest for life and a keen interest in books, language, art, travel, politics, and people, which made her a welcome guest at Bulstrode. Mrs Delany and the Duchess were charmed by this delightful girl whose manners and intelligence they found so pleasing. As by this time Mrs Delany's eyesight was failing Mary Hamilton used to read her letters and the newspaper to her. Together they walked or rode in a chaise in the park, with Mrs Delany wearing a pair of 'leathern shoes' which she had made herself some years earlier, returning mid-morning to eat oysters. The evenings were spent at their work-tables when Mrs Delany made cardboard trays for Mary Hamilton's collection of shells. The conversation was often of fashion and dress, but both the older ladies also liked to reminisce on the past. Mrs Delany spoke of the Hell Fire Club which she had heard about in her youth: 'It consisted of abt a dozen persons of fashion of both sexes, some of ye females unmarried, and the horrid impieties these were guilty of,' wrote Mary Hamilton recording the previous evening's conversation: 'they used to read and ridicule the Scriptures, and their conversation was blasphemous to ye last degree.' The Duchess of Portland had spoken of the extraordinary exploits of Sarah, Duchess of Marlborough, 'After the death of her granddaughter the Dss of Bedford, she was found one day lying prostrate on the ground, and a lady ... had like to have fallen over her, ye room being dark. Ye D. of M. said she was praying, and she lay thus upon the ground being too wicked to kneel.'

From Mary Hamilton too we hear of the negotiations between her uncle Sir William Hamilton, husband of Emma, and British

Ambassador to the Court of Naples, and the Duchess of Portland for the sale of the vase which was to become famous as the Portland Vase. Hamilton, a passionate collector of classical antiquities, had bought the vase in Italy for a thousand pounds, but as he was running into debt he was forced to sell it. His niece acted as a go-between in the negotiations and saved him the public embarrassment of trying to find a purchaser. Mrs Delany accompanied the Duchess twice to the hotel in King Street, St James's, to examine the vase, though her impaired sight forced her to hold the vase close to her face to see the fine details.

Of course two such remarkable old ladies must have been the subject of conversation amongst their friends. Sir William Hamilton exclaimed: 'Vive la vielle court, they are worth a million of the new-fangled ladies'. Dr Johnson said he had heard Edmund Burke, the orator, say of Mrs Delany 'she was the highest bred woman in the world, and the woman of fashion of all ages,' and, in a lighter vein, Horace Walpole, when asked by William Mason of news of the ladies replied, 'In the country fox-hunting.' From Mary Hamilton's diary we see her great affection for Mrs Delany: 'found the dear old woman in high beauty dressed in white sattin and her best lace cap, for her friend the Dss of Portland's birthday.' The secret of Mrs Delany's popularity may well have been her desire to make people feel valued for themselves. She shows this wish so often in her letters when receiving a gift: 'My affectionate wishes to my dear brother, and best thanks for the Oriental agate, the finest I ever saw; but that is the least part of its value to me.' She shows a particularly forgiving heart to her brother Bernard, who had become an intractable and grumpy bachelor: 'I must write to him, but with painful reluctance, as I never expect that cordiality which I feel I have a claim to, and cannot guess why it is withdrawn – but a stroke is given that cannot be entirely healed tho' I will apply all the lenients in my power.' At last in a time of great anxiety over the health of Mary Port soon after the birth of her daughter Georgina, Bernard shows his very real concern, commented upon by Lady Gower:

Tho' ye alarm may have been wt one may call a fiery tryal, on reflection it carries with it ye pleasing discovery of Mr Granville's *real affection*, wch from ye natural disposition of ye man (*if all went smooth*) might have laid dormant; this to dr Mrs Delany, who *wishes* every one to be wt they *ought to be*, must be a comfort.

Wherever Mrs Delany was, her company was sought eagerly, by family and friends, young and old, by famous and fashionable. What drew so many people to her even in old age is perhaps most eloquently expressed in the words of Hannah More, the reformer:

I spent a delightful day with Mrs Delany ... she is the object of my veneration, and I almost say envy. Such an excellent mind, so cultivated, such a tranquil grateful spirit, such a composed piety! She retains all that tenderness of heart which people are supposed to lose, and generally *do* lose in a very advanced age. She told me with some tears, that *she had no dread of death, but what arose from the thought how terribly her loss would be felt by one or two dear friends.*

7 *Flower Collage: a New Art*

'Scarlet Geranium' (in Mrs Delany's index this reads 'Bloody Cranesbill'). Probably her first 'paper mosaick', worked on shiny black paper.

It was during the period of her second widowhood, when Mrs Delany spent about half her time at Bulstrode, that she began her finest work of all. In the autumn of 1772 in her seventy-third year she wrote to her niece Mary Port, 'I have invented a new way of imitating flowers, I'll send you next time I write one for a sample.'

By continuing over the years to amuse herself and her friends with cut paper, Mrs Delany had developed remarkable skill with scissors. Through her needlework in particular, she had shown a love of plants combined with a superb sense of design and meticulous attention to detail. Her friendship with the Duchess of Portland had brought her into contact with some of the great botanists of the eighteenth century, and she built up a large store of botanical knowledge and appreciation. Her skill, her knowledge, her experience, and her artistry, reached their fulfilment in her flower collages. At an age when most people's powers are declining she created over a period of ten years a collection of nearly one thousand pictures of plants, made from paper, of botanical accuracy unsurpassed in that medium. The historical and social notes on the backs of the plant pictures greatly add to their value, making the collection an original herbarium.

Many years later Mrs Delany recalled how she had begun her new recreation. Sitting in her bedchamber at Bulstrode, she noticed the similarity of colour between a geranium and a piece of red paper that was on her table. Taking her scissors, she cut out the scarlet paper and, using more coloured paper for the leaves and stalk, she created a picture of a geranium. The Duchess on entering the room mistook the paper petals for real ones. Modest as she was, Mrs Delany considered her paper flowers to be a mere '*whim* of my own fancy' that 'might fondly beguile my judgement to think better of it than it deserved . . .', but the Duchess' enthusiasm encouraged her to persevere with her new art: 'Her approbation was such a sanction to my undertaking, as made it appear of consequence and gave me courage to go on with confidence.'

Today we would call Mrs Delany's pictures paper collage; she referred to them as 'paper mosaicks', and to her collection as her 'Herbal' or '*Hortus Siccus*'. She wrote later that her work was intended as an imitation of a *hortus siccus*, which is a collection of dried flowers. Such collections were popular at the time and it was typical of Mrs Delany's originality that her *hortus siccus* should be composed of paper flowers.

For Mrs Delany cutting her flowers of paper was more than merely a pleasurable pastime. After the death of Dr Delany there had been a gap in her life that she had not been able to fill. Her old enthusiasm for her previous activities was gone; the paper flowers were to be an '*employment* and *amusement*, to supply the loss of *those*, that had formerly been delightful to me; but had lost their power of pleasing; being deprived of that friend, whose partial approbation was my pride, and had stampt a value on them.' Mrs Delany now became absorbed in her flowers, and they gave her a fresh direction for her energies and a new challenge.

It is possible that Mrs Delany's venture into this medium was influenced by the seventeenth-century Turkish art of inserting flowers cut from coloured papers into the borders of manuscripts – if, in fact, she ever saw examples of these. Or she might have been influenced by the work of the Dietzsch family who often made drawings of flowers in opaque colours on deep brown or black paper. It is certain that at Bulstrode she knew the work of Ehret which the Duchess of Portland had commissioned. That and the drawings of other great botanical artists must have aroused her own creative powers, but it is likely that her flower collages began exactly as she described. Her quick eye for botanical detail, her highly developed colour sense and her gift of being able to cut out images as easily as she could draw them are enough to account for an invention which was probably fortuitous but which she developed into an art entirely her own.

With the plant specimen set before her she cut minute particles of coloured paper to represent the petals, stamens, calyx, leaves, veins, stalk and other parts of the plant, and, using lighter and darker paper to form the shading, she stuck them on to a black background. By placing one piece of paper upon another she sometimes built up several layers and in a complete picture there might be hundreds of pieces to form one plant. It is thought she first dissected each plant so that she might examine it carefully for accurate portrayal, certainly she displays not only an artist's eye but that of a botanist, as she included berries in 'Mespilus piracantha' (see p. 70), and the roots and bulb in 'Meadow Saffron' (see p. 130).

Initially she used a thin, shiny paper for background, but in 1774 she discarded this for a better matt surface, using paper which she obtained from a newly established paper-mill in Hampshire, and which she first washed with Indian ink. The dimensions of the background vary, but the plant is always cut to life size, by eye. The paper she used for the plants was procured from sailors who were bringing it from China, or obtained from paper-stainers (wall-paper manufacturers) whose colours had run; sometimes she dyed the paper herself to get the correct shade. Occasionally she touched up the pictures with watercolour after sticking the paper into position, but this was the exception rather than the rule. It is uncertain what glue she used to stick down the paper, possibly egg-white or flour and water, as a laboratory test on one picture has detected a starch-based agent. Each picture has her initials MD generally in a corner below the plant, always cut in paper in one piece, although the style of the initial may vary.

Mrs Delany's skill in cutting paper in the first three years was shown by the 'Feather'd Pink' (see illustration), also by 'Willow-Leav'd Dogsbane' (*Trachomitum venetum*) where the casing of the pod has 114 spines individually cut, and by the fine strips of lighter paper which edge the petals of 'Jacobean Lily' (see p. 160). The earliest pictures are numbered on the back up to fifty-two but then instead she began to record the day, month and year that each one was completed. These dates are of particular botanical interest because her pictures included some of the seven thousand plants which arrived in Britain in the eighteenth century, brought back by explorers not only as proof of reaching the unexplored world but for their economic, scientific and medicinal value. She also wrote the place where she had worked the picture, generally either her home in St James's Place, or Bulstrode, and occasionally added a social note, 'Lady Weymouth at Bulstrode', or 'Mr Montague and Mr Mason here'. By the end of 1775 she had created over one hundred pictures.

By this time her skills had reached their peak. With the greater use of varying shades of paper she had virtually eliminated the need

'Dianthus superbus, Feather'd Pink'. Numbered 22 on the back.

Detail of 'Passeflora Laurifolia' (see p. 72). the bloom includes 230 paper petals.

to use watercolour and the pictures began to be made of hundreds of finely-cut snippets of coloured paper. There is more movement in the plants, with leaves curled to show the lighter shades beneath, and paper cut with hair-like precision for the veins and stamens, giving a more life-like appearance to the plants.

In April 1776 Mrs Delany wrote from her house in St James's Place to her niece: 'The spring flowers now supply me with work, for I have already done since the beginning of March 20 plants.' It had become her habit to start her 'paper mosaicks' after breakfast. However, there were often callers to interrupt her hobby. Lady Bute brought the Duchess of Gordon to meet Mrs Delany for the first time under the pretence of showing the Duchess Mrs Delany's Herbal, but 'really to treat me with her beauty. She is beautiful indeed, is very natural and good humour'd but her very broad Scotch accent does not seem to belong to the very great delicacy of her appearance.' Sometimes a direct reference to a plant was made in a letter as, for example, to Viscountess Andover who was so skilled at cutting landscapes that a magnifying glass was needed to appreciate her intricate workmanship. Mrs Delany wrote 'I have been at my usual presumption of copying beautiful nature: I have bungled out a horse chestnut blossom that would make a fine figure in a lady's cap'—an indication of the fashions of the day. Her friend Mrs Boscawen had Mrs Delany's botanical hobby much in mind when she wrote of a yellow carnation in her hot-house: 'How perfectly you would represent it' and later Mrs Boscawen wrote 'is this Indian paper good for anything to you, my dear madam. It is real Indian . . . I have half a dozen sheets more if this would be any use to you.'

The fame of Mrs Delany's *hortus siccus* spread beyond her own circle. One day in the summer of 1776 the King drove the Queen in a little low chaise the half-hour journey from Windsor to Bulstrode, accompanied by Lady Weymouth, her lady-in-waiting, who was one of the Duchess's daughters. It was an expected but informal visit to drink tea and they arrived between six and seven in the evening. Mrs Delany wrote:

All things were prepared for their reception, and the drawing room divested of every comfortable circumstance. I pleaded hard with her Grace for permission to go that day to London; she was inexorable; but I still had hopes that so insignificant a person would be over-looked, and that I should be fully gratified with seeing their royalties thro' ye windows, or thro' the keyhole. But I was mistaken, and Lady Weymouth was sent by the Queen to desire I would bring the *Hortus Siccus*.

This was the beginning of a friendship between Mrs Delany and the royal family that was to last until the end of her life. The King and Queen became frequent callers at Bulstrode, often unexpected and even unannounced. Mrs Delany described the stir that one such visit caused in 1783, soon after the birth of Princess Amelia, the last of their fifteen children:

The Dss of Portland and I were sitting in the long gallery very busy with our different employments, when, without ceremony, his Majesty walked up to our table, *un*perceived and *un*known till he came quite close to us. You may believe we were at first a little fluttered, but his courteous manner soon made him a welcome guest. He came to inform the Duchess of Portland of the Queen's perfect recovery after her lying-in, which made him doubly welcome.

The King stayed for two hours, an indication of the pleasure he took in their company. Another time the King and Queen brought five of the princesses: 'They were all dressed in white muslin polinises, white chip hats, with white feathers, except the Queen who had on a black hat and cloak . . . the King was in his Windsor uniform blue and gold.' The Queen gave Mrs Delany a frame for weaving fringe:

. . . of a new and most delicate structure . . . you will easily imagine the grateful feeling I had when the Queen presented it to me, to make up some knotted fringe which she saw me about . . . the King at the same time said he must contribute something to my work and presented me with a gold knotting shuttle of most exquisite workmanship and taste; and I am at this time, while dictating, knotting white silk to fringe the bag which is to contain it.

These gifts were in addition to a locket given her by the Queen containing a tress of the Queen's hair with crown and cypher on the back, and a necklace with a locket containing a miniature of the King, set in gold and diamonds. Etiquette demanded that these royal visits should be returned by a personal call to Windsor Castle to enquire after the welfare of their Majesties, and Mrs Delany accompanied the Duchess whenever she was able. There were many invitations to the ladies to spend an evening at the Queen's Lodge in the castle grounds to listen to a concert or hear Mrs Siddons reading from *The Provoked Husband*.

The King and Queen were both interested in botany, and at the Royal Botanic Gardens at Kew plants were grown that were new to Britain. It was after the King and Queen had made a visit to Bulstrode and admired her paper mosaicks that Mrs Delany recorded 'Kew' on the back of her pictures; it was presumably by direct command of their Majesties that plants were sent from Kew for her to copy. Sir Joseph Banks had been in charge of the gardens since 1772, and would have been pleased to send her the eighty-four plants which she received. A letter to her niece in 1777 indicates the steady flow: 'I am so *plentifully* supplied with the hot-house here, and from the Queen's garden at Kew, that natural plants have been a good deal laid aside this year for foreigners, but not less in favour.'

Another botanical garden that was to supply Mrs Delany with many plants was the Chelsea Physic Garden, nearly a hundred years older than the Royal Botanic Gardens at Kew. She must have recalled with pleasure Philip Miller's visits to Bulstrode during his fifty years in charge of Chelsea. Miller was particularly successful at germinating seeds sent to him by a large number of correspondents. He distributed plants to other botanic and private gardens; cotton seeds were sent out to the new colony at Georgia and became the staple crop, and in return seeds of new species were received from the Americas. Mrs Delany copied fourteen plants from Chelsea, including the magnificent 'Tree Aloe' (*Aloe barbadensis*).

Mrs Delany's skill extended to knotting (or tatting) and this was acknowledged by George III by his gift to Mrs Delany of this gold knotting shuttle.

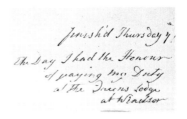

Mrs Delany's note 'finished Thursday y.ᵉ [1] The Day I had the Honour of paying my Duty at the Queen's Lodge at Windsor', written on the back of 'Jatropha multifida, Scarlet-flower'd Physic-nut'.

'Rosa Gallica var. Blush Rose', showing insect bite cut in leaf.

‘Hibiscus Rosa Sinensis, China Rose’

In August 1776 she paid two short visits, the first was to Lord and Lady Bute at Luton Park. Lord Bute, one time Prime Minister, was a keen horticulturalist and grew many interesting plants at Luton. Mrs Delany was fond of Lady Bute so it was always a pleasure for her to go there. In a brief visit of three or four days she portrayed ‘Scarlet Blood Flower’ (*Haemanthus coccineus*) and ‘Blue African Crinum’ (*Agapanthus umbellatus*) she then moved on to Lady Gower’s at Bill Hill, near Reading, with ‘Blue Garden Chich Vetch’, (*Larythus sativus*, ‘chichling vetch’) and ‘Climbing fumetory’ (see p. 41) from the garden at Luton, crammed in the tin box in which she conveyed her precious plants. At Bill Hill, in a single week, she completed not only the two plants from Luton, but also another five from Lady Gower’s garden. One of these was a flower taken from a magnolia tree (see p. 32), much admired by the two ladies; some years later Lady Gower wrote to Mrs Delany, ‘Mother Magnolia and all her daughters have been in full bloom this month past.’ As Mrs Delany pasted down the cream-coloured paper to represent the petals of the magnolia she may have recalled that Ehret had walked the three miles between Chelsea and Parson’s Green in Fulham

RIGHT ‘Clethra Alnifolia’ (in her index Mrs Delany wrote ‘Virginian Cat’s Tail’), and FAR RIGHT a detail of the left-hand spray. A real leaf is included in this picture, lower right. This flower was completed during a visit to Bill Hill.

'Mimosa latisiliqua, White flowering accasia wth broad pods' [*Lysiloma latisiliqua*]. Over 500 leaves are cut in various shades of green.

almost daily in order to watch a magnolia grandiflora unfold its magnificent buds in Sir Charles Wager's garden in 1733, when the tree was new to this country. The work that she did on these two occasions indicates she travelled about with her cutting implements and paper; what an easy guest she must have been for her hostesses, who knew she would be happily employed whatever the weather.

In the autumn Mrs Delany continued her work at Bulstrode with even greater speed, writing happily to Mary Port: 'We are alone, save Mr Lightfoot, and we are as busy as bees.' She excelled with the

'Carduus nutans, Musk or
nodding Thistle'

'White flowering accasia' (see illustration), with its 543 leaves and
120 stamens in one bloom alone, as well as showing pod and seeds,
and in 'Musk or nodding Thistle' (see illustration), its leaves
swirling like waves in a turbulent sea.

After spending the first five months of 1777 in London, Mrs
Delany moved to Bulstrode where the extent of her Herbal
immediately increased. There was the 'Burnet Rose' (see p. 108)
with thorns of various sizes on the stalks, followed the next day by
the dainty 'Wood Strawberry' (see p. 42). Sometimes she included a

142

(see p. 148)

LEFT 'Solanum Melongena, Egg Plant'. Finely cut strips of lighter paper edge the leaves. This plant was growing in the hot-house at Bulstrode.

real part of a plant, generally one or two leaves, or, as in her 'Dog Rose' (*Rosa canina*), a small sprig of leaves; in the 'Winter Cherry' (see p. 148) she used the real skeleton of a pod case to stick over the paper seeds. Only one picture contains a real flower: a floret of 'Scarlet Flower'd Heath' (*Erica cruenta?*), one of a collection of ericas which had come from the Cape of Good Hope.

The speed with which Mrs Delany worked at her pictures was truly amazing. In October of the same year she created twenty-eight, a record for one month. She wrote to Mary Port:

Now I know you smile, and say what can take up so much of A.D.'s [Aunt Delany's] time? No children to teach or play with; no house matters to torment her; no books to publish; no politicks to work her brains? All this is true but idleness never grew in my soil, tho' I can't boast of any very useful employments, only such as keep me from being a burthen to my friends, and banish the spleen; and therefore are as important for the present use as matters of higher nature.

Many of the collages were of flowers from the garden or hot-house at Bulstrode but as her skill became known, plants were sent to her from many sources. In 1778 there is a variety of names amongst the donors of plants, noted on the back of her pictures. Lord Dartmouth, Secretary for Trade and the Plantations, gave her 'Turnsole' (*Heliotropium peruvianum*); Mrs Astley, her waiting-woman, brought her 'Double Flowering Peach' (*Prunus persica*) from Barnes; Lord Rockingham, one-time Prime Minister, presented her with 'Asphodil Lilly' (*Crinum latifolium* var. *zeylanicum*); from Lord Willoughby's marsh garden came 'Dwarf Almond Amygdalus nana' (*Prunus tenella*) and from Lord Mansfield she received 'Cassia Marylandica', which he probably brought from his garden at Kenwood.

She was unwell in the summer of 1778 and in July wrote to Mary Port of her returning health and of a visit to Lord and Lady Bute:

I have for some weeks past been a sort of rambler in a little compass trying my wings for a longer flight, if my strength will allow me. I spent my time at Luton very agreeably, but more of magnificence than comfort belongs to that place, except in the very kind and obliging manner I was received by the owners, who had every consideration for me, to make my situations as easy as possible, and a curious and enquiring mind can't fail of being gratified there, as well as at Bulstrode.

So meticulous was Mrs Delany in portraying the plants accurately that she took great care to cut the correct number of stamens and styles, and this was recorded on the back of most of her pictures using the Linnaean sexual system of classification. Carl

OVERLEAF

LEFT Pancratium Maritinum, Sea Daffodil'. The anthers at the end of the stamens are shown clearly.

RIGHT 'Cactus Grandiflorus, Melon Thistle' [*Selenicereus grandiflorus*]. On the back is written 'Bulstrode 12 August 1778 The Day the King and Queen and the Royal Family were at Bulstrode'.

Linnaeus (1707-78), the Swedish doctor and scientist, was one of the great naturalists of that century. The system he had devised was widely used between 1737 and 1810. He divided all flowering plants into twenty-three classes based on the male organs, that is according to the number of stamens: Monandria has one stamen, Diandria two stamens, Triandria three stamens and so on. These classes were further divided into orders based on the female organs: Monogynia with one style or sessile stigma, Digynia with two styles or sessile stigmas, Trigynia with three, and so on. Thus on the back of both 'Jacobean Lily' (see p. 160) and 'Sea Daffodil' (see p. 144) Mrs Delany has written Hexandria Monogynia, the six stamens and one style have been cut with such dexterity that even the anther at the end of the stamens, and the stigma on the style are shown.

In July 1778 Dr Solander made a return visit to Bulstrode accompanied by the Swedish botanist and explorer Claz Alstroemer (1736–96), after whom the Peruvian Lilly (*Alstroemeria*) is named; their visit is recorded on the back of the 'Stewartia Malacodendron' together with the date and a note that the flower came from Kew. She wrote to Mary Port: 'Dr Solander etc came, as expected and I am now going to get a botanical lecture and to copy a beautiful flower called Stuartia.'

One of her most magnificent pictures is the 'Melon Thistle' (see previous page). The bloom is made up of 190 parts and 399 spines protrude from the stem, which itself is composed of ten shades of paper. On the back she wrote, 'Bulstrode 12 August 1778, The Day the King and Queen and the Royal Family were at Bulstrode.' This was one of the formal Royal visits, and is described in a letter to her niece:

The order in which the King and Queen and Royal Family with their attendants, went from Windsor to breakfast with the Duchess Dowager of Portland at Bulstrode, on Wednesday the 12th of August, 1778 the Prince of Wales birthday.

2 Servants on horseback
The Prince of Wales and Prince Frederick on horseback
General Budé and Montagu, Riding Master
2 Footmen and 2 Grooms
King and Queen in a phaeton and pair
2 Servants on horseback
A postchaise and 4 horses, in which were the Princess Royal, Prince Adolphus the King's seventh son and Lady Weymouth
2 Servants on horseback

'Stewartia Malacodendron'

146

LEFT 'Physalis, Winter Cherry'

RIGHT 'Tamus communis, Black Briony'. A real leaf is included, lower centre.

A coach and six horses, in which were Princess Augusta, Princess Elizabeth, Lady Charlotte Finch, the Governess to the Royal children, and Miss Goldworthy, 2 footmen behind

A coach and six horses, in which were Prince William, Prince Edward, the Bishop of Lichfield and Mr Arnold Sub Precentor, 2 footman behind.

2 Servants on horseback

A coach and six horses, in which were Mr Hotham, Mr Smelt, Mr Lake, Mr Light, 2 Servants behind the coach

2 Servants on horseback

A phaeton in which were the Duke of Montagu and General Fretock. N.B. The Duke of Montagu's phaeton went before the last coach and 6. Each coach had a helper besides footmen and grooms, in all 33 servants, and 56 personages.

Before 12 o'clock the cavalcade drove into the court, the Dss Dr of Portland ready on the stone steps at the hall door to receive her royal guests. I was below stairs in my own apartment not dress'd and uncertain if I should be thought of. But down came Lady Weymouth (with her pretty eyes sparkling) with the Queen's commands that I should attend her, which I did. The Queen most graciously came up to me and the 3 princesses. The King and the 2 eldest princes were in the dining-room looking at the pictures, but soon came in, and then they all went in a train thro' the great apartment to the Duchess of Portland's china closet, and with wondering and enquiring eyes admired all her magnificent curiosities. They staid above half an hour, and I took that time to take breath and sit down quietly in the drawing-room; when they returned the Queen sat down, and called me to her to talk about the chenille work, praising it much more than it deserved, but with a politeness that could not fail of giving pleasure, and indeed her manners are most engaging, there is so much dignity and affability blended that it is hard to say whether one's respect or love predominates. The Duchess of Portland brought her Majesty a dish of tea, roles and cakes . . . everything proper for the time of day was prepared, tea, chocolate and bread and butter . . . and on another table all sorts of fruit and ice . . . The King drank chocolate and was all good spirits and good humour.

The King asked me if I had added to my book of flowers, and desiring he might see it. It was placed on a table before the Queen, who was attended by the Princess Royal and the rest of ye ladies, the King standing and looking over them. I kept my distance, till the Queen called me to answer some question about a flower, when I came, and the King brought a chair and set it at the table, opposite to the Queen, and graciously took me by the hand and seated me in it, an honour I could not receive without some confusion and hesitation: 'Sit down, sit down,' said her Majesty, 'it is not everybody has a chair brought them by a king.'

The following day Mrs Delany copied 'Pomegranate' (*Punica granatum* var. *nana*) and wrote on the back, 'Bulstrode 13th August 1778 The Day after their Majesties, the Prince of Wales, the Bishop

'Camellia Japonica'

Alfred. Oclav. Soph.Mary. Adolph. Aug. Eliz.Ern.   Soph.Aug.   Edw.   PfRoy. W.Hen.   Fred.   P.Wales   Charl. Geo.III.
died.Aug1782.

Amelia
born Aug 9, 1783.   1781.

of Osnaburg and the three younger Princes, Princess Royal, Princess Augusta and Princess Elizabeth had been at Bulstrode.'

One week later the Queen is recorded as the donor of a carnation (*Dianthus caryophyllus*). The carnation was by far the oldest of the florist's flowers and had been cultivated in England since at least the fourteenth century. It was the latest of the florist's flowers to bloom, and the only one to have much fragrance; in the days when dahlias, chrysanthemums and michaelmas daisies were still unknown it was to many gardeners the final important flower of the year. 'For my part,' wrote William Cobbett in the *American Gardener* (1821), 'as a thing to keep and not to sell; as a thing the possession of which is to give me pleasure, I hesitate not a moment to prefer the plant of a fine carnation, to a gold watch set with diamonds.'

Mrs Delany, who had always delighted in sharing her pleasures, was as generous as ever with her paper flowers, and friends received pictures as presents. To Mrs Anne Viney, a friend who had moved to Gloucester, she sent two pictures, but, she warns, 'allowance must be made that it is the work of an old woman, nearly ent'ring into her

A pen and wash drawing of George III and Queen Charlotte walking in procession with their fourteen children, dated 1781 (Amelia, their youngest child, was not yet born).

8oth year. You will have my dog-rose and jessamine a little sooner but it has been a week so filled with Royal favours that it allowed me no leisure for anything else. I like my new servant (Lydia Rea) very much, she is sensible, lively, and attentive, and she reads aloud very well, which is very comfortable to me.' The Countess of Stamford, another of the Duchess of Portland's daughters, so connected botany with Mrs Delany that when the name of the new servant caught her eye she 'thought Lydia Rea was a curious new type of flower—it look'd Linnaean.'

Mrs Delany was back again at her house in London for the winter months and was looking after her great-niece Georgina Port, then aged seven. From 1778 Georgina regularly came to stay with her aunt in London. Mrs Delany delighted in the company of her young great-niece, whom she took under her wing. She supervised her education, and took her on her many visits, introducing Georgina into her social circle. George Keate, a poet and friend of Mrs Delany wrote of her influence on Georgina:

With that benevolence which condescends
   To guide its knowledge to the youthful heart
O'er thee, my child, the good Delany bends
   Directs thy scissors, and reveals her art.

Ah seize the happy moment! she can show
   The mazy path mysterious Nature treads
Can steal her varied grace, her varied glow
   And all the changeful beauties that she spreads.

Then mark the kind instructress, watch her hand
   Her judgement, her inspiring touch attain;
Thy scissors make, like hers, a majic wand;
   Tho' much I fear thy efforts will be in vain.

Failing in this my child forbear the strife;
   Another path to fame by her is shown;—
Try by thy pattern of her honour'd life,
   With equal virtue to cut thine own.

Mrs Delany wrote to Georgina's mother in the spring of 1779, of their call on the Quaker and philanthropist John Fothergill:

I am so busy now with rare plants from all my botanical friends, and idle visitors and my little charge must have a share of my time that it generally drives my writing to candlelight, which does not suit my age-worn eyes. Last Thursday I took my little bird and Mrs Pott to Upton in Essex, 10 miles off, to Dr Fothergill's garden, crammed my tin box with exoticks, overpowered with such variety I knew not what to chuse! Georgina delighted fluttered about like a newborn butterfly.

Mrs Delany came away with six plants which she copied into her collage collection. Dr Fothergill's famous garden contained the finest range of ornamental and useful plants from all over the world. Sir Joseph Banks said: 'at an expense seldom undertaken by an individual, Dr Fothergill procured from all parts of the world a great number of the rarest plants and protected them in the amplest buildings which this or any other country has seen'.

Another day they went for 'an airing to the Physic Garden at Chelsea ... We returned loaded with the spoyls of the Botanical Garden. Georgina was surprised at a live chameleon she saw in a hot-house.' Sometimes they went to Islington where the physician Dr Pitcairn gave Mrs Delany many plants from his garden of five acres; at other times they journeyed to the Lee and Kennedy nursery garden at Hammersmith:

I am just returned from a pleasant tour this morning with your dear child – we went to Lee's at Hammersmith in search of flowers, but only met with a crinum, a sort of Pancratium Crinum Asiaticum, from there returned to Kensington, bought cheesecakes, buns, etc, a whole 18 pennyworth; from thence to a lane that leads to Brompton, and are now come home hungry as hawks, dinner ready, and we must dress.

James Lee was one of the great gardeners of the day; after leaving the employment of the Duke of Northumberland at Sion, Middlesex, he had entered into partnership with Lewis Kennedy at the Vineyards, Hammersmith. There they opened a nursery garden where they grew exotic plants, including the first seeds from Botany Bay. Lee gave Mrs Delany many plants, including 'Scarlet Flower'd Ipomea' (see p. 1) which, not being hardy, must have grown in one of Lee's extensive greenhouses.

Georgina returned to her mother for the summers but she was kept fully informed of Mrs Delany's social life, especially royal visits:

The Queen was dress'd in a embroider'd lutestring; Princess Royal in deep orange or scarlet, I could not by candlelight distinguish which, Pss Augusta in pink, Pss Elizabeth in blue; these were all in robes without aprons. Princess Mary (a most sweet child) was in cherry-colour'd tabby, with silver leading strings; she is about four years old; she cou'd not remember my name, but, making me a very low curtsey, she said, 'How do you do, Duchess of Portland's friend; and how does your little niece do. I wish you had brought her.' The King carried about in his arms by turns Princess Sophia, and the last Prince, Octavius ... I never saw more lovely children, for a more pleasing sight than the King's fondness for them, and the Queen's; for they seem to have but *one mind*, and that is to make everything easy and happy about them. The King brought in his arms the little Octavius prince to me, who held out his hand to play with me, which, on my taking the liberty to kiss, his M. made him kiss my cheek . . . we staid till past 11; came home by a charming moon; did not sup till past 12, nor in bed till *two*. Now don't you think my dearest G.M.A. [Georgina Mary Anne] that A.D. was a great rake? . . .

In July 1779, Mrs Delany wrote an introduction to her *Hortus Siccus*, which she placed at the beginning of the first volume. It was headed: 'Plants, Copied after Nature in paper Mosaick begun in the year 1774.' She probably considered her first efforts in 1772 and 1773 were not worth recording, although some were kept and placed in her volumes. She continued with an acknowledgement to her friend the Duchess of Portland who had given her so much encouragement in this work:

To *her* I owe the spirit of pursuing it with diligence and pleasure. To *her* I owe more than I dare express, but my heart will ever feel with the utmost gratitude, and tenderest affection, the honour, and delight I have enjoy'd in her most generous, steady, and delicate friendship, for above forty years.

These two introductory pages include a verse:

> Hail to the happy hour! when fancy led
> My Pensive mind this flo'ry path to tread;
> And gave me emulation to presume
> With timid art, to trace fair Natures bloom:
> To view with awe the great Creative Power,
> That shines confess'd in the minutest flower;
> With wonder to pursue the Glorious line
> And gratefully adore The Hand Divine!

It was after the Queen and three of the Princesses had made one of their many informal calls to Bulstrode that we get a hint of the tools that Mrs Delany used. 'The Queen sate down to my working table,' she wrote, 'view'd all my implements, look'd over a volume of the plants, and made me sit down by her all the time.' When the Royal party left the Queen handed a gift to Mrs Delany as she was returning to London for some months. The incident was described by Mrs Delany's waiting-woman: 'Inside was a beautiful pocket case, the outside satin work'd with gold and ornaments with gold spangles, the inside lined with pink satin and contained a knife, sizsars, pencle, rule, compass, bodkin.' A bodkin was used when she worked the 'Eatable Wake Robin' (see p. 156) where holes of varying sizes have been pierced in yellow paper in the pistil to reveal off-white paper beneath. But of other tools she gives us no idea

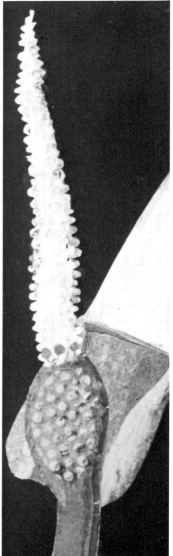

except referring to scissors. At one end of the packet was a pocket containing a letter from the Queen written in her own hand. The envelope addressed to Mrs Delany measured approximately $2 \times 2\frac{3}{4}$ inches, inside in neat handwriting the Queen wrote:

Without appearing imprudent towards Mrs Delany, and indiscreet to her friends who wish to preserve her as her excellent qualities well deserve, I cannot have the pleasure of enjoying her company this winter with which our amiable friend the Duchess Dowager of Portland has so frequently and politely indulged me with during the summer. I must therefore desire that

ABOVE LEFT 'Arum esculentum, Eatable Wake Robin [*Colocasia esculenta*]. From a drawing of Lady Anne Monson's – Madras', and ABOVE detail of pistil, showing holes in yellow paper, probably made with a bodkin.

Queen Charlotte's letter to Mrs
Delany, 15 December 1781.

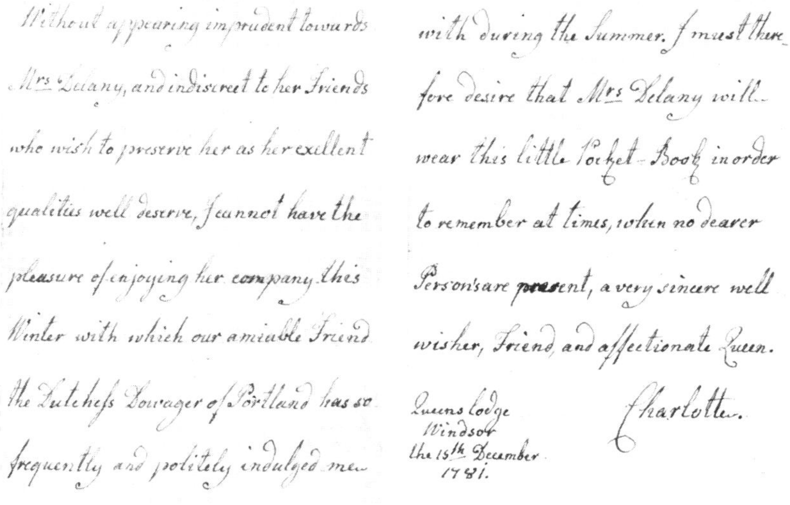

[Handwritten letter reproduced in image]

Mrs Delany will wear this little pocket book in order to remember at times,
when no dearer persons are present, a very sincere wellwisher, friend and
affectionate Queen.

CHARLOTTE

Queen's Lodge
Windsor
the 15th December 1781

Sadly the Queen's gift arrived just at the time when Mrs Delany's
eyesight was beginning to fail. She continued with her collages for
the next year, producing among others 'Meadowsweet' (*Filipendula
ulmaria*) with minute white petals, and 'Bombax Ceiba' (see p. 159),
which was copied from a painting by the intrepid traveller Lady
Anne Monson (*c.* 1714–76). But in her eighty-third year her
eyesight deteriorated rapidly and, always a perfectionist, she laid
down her scissors.

The success of Mrs Delany's 'paper mosaicks' inspired other
ladies to try their hands, and among those to whom she gave
instruction was Miss Jennings, 'a sensible agreeable, and ingenious
woman a pupil of mine in the paper mosaick work (and the only one
I have any hopes of) came here last Thursday.' A few of Mrs
Delany's pictures worked in the last years have 'begun by Mrs
Delany and finished by Miss Jennings' written on the back.

Ten large volumes contain the pictures, nine with one hundred
each, and the tenth with seventy-two. Each volume is indexed with
botanical and common names written in her clear hand.

There were many tributes to this superb herbarium: amongst the artists, Sir Joshua Reynolds acknowledged them as unrivalled in perfection and outline, delicacy of cutting, accuracy of shading and perspective, harmony and brilliancy of colours. They were also the admiration of botanists, Sir Joseph Banks remarking that they were the only representations of nature he had ever seen from which he could venture to describe botanically any plant without the least fear of committing an error. Erasmus Darwin, grandfather of Charles, added his praise, and Horace Walpole referred to her collage in *Anecdotes of Painters*, mentioning Mrs Delany as 'a lady of excellent sense and taste, who painted in oil, and who invented the art of paper mosaic, with material (coloured) she executed . . . 20 of 1000 various flowers and flowering shrubs with a precision and truth unparalleled.' He gave her a new edition of the book and told her she had founded a new branch of painting.

With poignant words Mrs Delany takes leave of her flowers:

A FAREWELL
The time has come! I can no more
The vegetable world explore;
No more with rapture cull each flower
That paints the mead or twines the bower;
No more with admiration see
Its beauteous form and symmetry;
No more attempt with hope elate
Its lovely hues to imitate!
Farewell! to all those friendly powers
That blest my solitary hours;
Alas! Farewell! but shall I mourn
As one who is of hope forlorn?
Ah no! My mind with rapture feels
The promise which Thy word reveals
Come Holy Spirit, on thy wing
Thy sacred consolation bring
Teach me to contemplate that grace
Which hath so long sustained my race;
Which various blessings still bestows,
And pours in balm to all my woes!
O sanctify the pointed dart
That at this moment rends my heart;
Teach me submissive to resign
When summoned by Thy Will Divine.

St James's Place, May 1782.

'Bombax Ceiba Linn spec. 959. From a drawing of Lady Anne Monson'.

8　*Their Majesties' Friend*

In July 1785, the Dowager Duchess of Portland died at Bulstrode after only a few days' illness. It was completely unexpected and a great shock to Mrs Delany. Apart from the loss of her companion it meant that she no longer had her summer retreat to go to at Bulstrode, but the King offered her a little house at Windsor, to which she moved in September 1785. The house was fully furnished and she received the following letter from Queen Charlotte when it was ready:

My dear Mrs Delany will be glad to hear that I am charged by the King to summon her to her new abode at Windsor for Tuesday next, when she will find all the most essential part of the house ready, excepting some little trifles that it will be better for Mrs Delany to direct herself in person or by her little deputy, Miss Port. I need not, I hope, add that I shall be extremely glad and happy to see so amiable an inhabitant in this our sweet retreat, and wish very sincerely that our dear Mrs Delany may enjoy every blessing among us that her merits deserve, and that we may long enjoy her amiable company. Amen. These are the true sentiments of my dear Mrs Delany's very affectionate queen.

CHARLOTTE

The welcome Mrs Delany received from the King and Queen on her arrival at the little house in St Alban's Street set the pattern for her relationship with them for the remaining three years of her life:

I arrived here about eight o'clock in the evening and found His Majesty in the house ready to receive me. I threw myself at his feet, indeed unable to say a word, he raised and saluted me, and said he meant not to stay longer than to desire I would *order everything* that could make the house comfortable and agreeable to me, and then retired. Truly I found *nothing wanting*, as it is as pleasant and commodious as I could wish it to be, with a *very pretty garden*, which joins to that of the Queen's Lodge.

'Jacobean Lily, Amaryllis formossissima' [*Sprekelia formosissima*]

The Queen gave her welcome in a letter written in her own hand:

My dearest Mrs Delany

   If coming to me will not fatigue your spirits *too* much I shall receive you with open arms, and am

Your affectionate friend

CHARLOTTE

Windsor Castle, a print after George Robertson. George III and Queen Charlotte walk with their Court on the terrace, with the newly built Queen's Lodge in the background.

Unable to go to the Queen's Lodge, Mrs Delany received the Queen in her upstairs drawing-room, both of them aware it was the first time of their meeting since the death of the Dowager Duchess of Portland.

I was lame, and therefore could not go down to the door; but her Majesty came upstairs. Our meeting was mutually affecting; she well knew the value of what I had lost, and it was sometime after we were seated (for she always makes me sit down), before we could either of us speak. She repeated in the strongest terms her wish, and the King's that I should be as easy and as happy as *they could possibly make me*; and they waved all ceremony, and desired to come to me like *friends*! The Queen also delivered a paper from the King, it contained the first quarter of £300 per annum, which his Majesty allows me out of his privy purse. Their Majesties have drunk tea with me five times and the Princesses three. They generally stay two hours or longer. In short I have either seen or heard of them every day, but I have not yet been at the Queen's Lodge, though they have expressed impatience for me to come, as I have still so sad a drawback upon my spirits that I must decline that honour till I am better able to enjoy it, as they have the goodness not to *press me*. Their visits here are paid in the most quiet manner, like those of the most consoling and interested friends; so that I may *truly* say, they are a *royal cordial*.

The royal visitors would drop into her house at any time of the day, sometimes coming in the morning, 'when they take me as I am'. Or the Queen might arrive mid-day for a couple of hours, inviting Mrs Delany to join them at the Queen's Lodge the same evening. On occasions both the King and Queen walked in unannounced, which, though evidence of their fondness for her, must at times have been disconcerting both for Mrs Delany and Georgina. Once when Mrs Delany and Georgina were eating their dinner the Queen arrived and sat down to enjoy the orange pudding with them, and finding it delicious she requested the recipe. Unfortunately the Royal cooks seemed unable to make it so well

After Dr Delany's death, Mrs Delany took a house in London, firstly in Thatched House Court; she later moved to St James's Place. This print shows a view of St James's Square, dated 1768.

and thereafter it was cooked at Mrs Delany's house and sent over to the Queen's Lodge.

After a few weeks, and feeling in better spirits, Mrs Delany accepted invitations to join the King and Queen and their family. The King had great respect for her age and would greet her with, 'Come along, Mrs Delany', and invite her to lean on his arm. She normally arrived about seven o'clock for an evening of family enjoyment. She described the domestic scene:

I have been several evenings at the Queen's Lodge, with no other company but their own most lovely family. They sit round a large table, on which are books, work, pencils and paper. The Queen has the goodness to make me sit down next to her; and delights me with her conversation, which is informing, elegant, and pleasing, beyond description; whilst the younger

George III and his family at Windsor by the Victorian artist Henrietta Ward (1832–1924), depicting a scene of simple domesticity which Mrs Delany describes in a letter. She sits with Queen Charlotte, on the right.

A game of chess, and a lady tambouring. The man on the far left is probably Thomas Thynne, third Viscount Weymouth, later first Marquess of Bath. A silhouette cut by Mrs Delany.

part of the family are drawing and working, &.&, the beautiful babe, Princess Amelia, bearing her part in the entertainment sometimes in one of her sisters' laps; sometimes playing with the King on the carpet; which, altogether, exhibits such a delightful scene as would require an Addison's pen or a Vandyke pencil, to do justice to it.

Mrs Delany's day began with prayers at eight o'clock in the King's chapel, which the King and Queen and their family attended; she was carried there in an elegant sedan chair given her by the King expressly for the purpose. Breakfast was at nine, followed by the necessary business of running the house. After that she often went for an airing in her chaise for two hours; at other times she received callers, sometimes as many as nine in a morning, among them Dr Hurd, Bishop of Worcester, Dr Richard Pulteney a physician and botanist, and Dr Joseph Warton, Headmaster of Winchester College, who was famous for daring to rebuke Dr Johnson when they met at Sir Joshua Reynolds's house. (Dr Johnson had said that he was 'not used to being contradicted', and Dr Warton replied that 'it would be better if he were'.) Mrs Delany found Dr Warton a delightful companion and wrote of him to Mary Port: 'I wish he resided at Westminster and not Winchester, that I might enjoy more of his sprightly and edifying conversation.' Another caller was the Rev. W. Gilpin, author of *Observations on Forest Scenery*, who requested he might bring Mrs Gilpin to see the 'Flora Delanica', as Mrs Delany jokingly called her collection of plant pictures.

Mrs Delany's intimacy with the royal family was encouraged by the many interests they had in common. The King was musical, and shared Mrs Delany's admiration for Handel's compositions; she was pleased to lend him manuscripts that had been left by Handel in his will to her brother Bernard. The King's pleasure in his Botanic Garden at Kew was another interest she shared with him, and as she had shown some enthusiasm for astronomy at Bulstrode she must surely have discussed William Herschel's telescope, which he had erected at Slough a few miles away and which the King had been to see.

The Queen was well-read in English, German, and French, and sometimes lent books to Mrs Delany. Needlework, drawing and painting were all pastimes she enjoyed, and she encouraged her daughters to follow the same pursuits. At the invitation of the Queen, Mrs Delany designed chair seats for her; the pattern of leaves was to be cut in satin in several shades of brown and to be sewn on to a blue background.

Undoubtedly Mrs Delany inspired the Queen and the Princesses with her flower collages. The Queen became a keen botanist, and pressed flowers on to black paper when creating her 'Herbal', which must have received Mrs Delany's encouragement. Princess Elizabeth was taught to cut silhouettes by Mrs Delany, which she developed to a high standard. The recent reappearance at Windsor Castle of a booklet of silhouettes cut by Mrs Delany gives further proof of their mutual esteem. The frontispiece shows the King, full length in profile, with sword, and opposite the Queen has written:

This elegant little book was given to me by Mrs Delany on 13th November 1781 at Bullstrode in the presence of Her Amiable Friend the Dutchess Dowager of Portland.

CHARLOTTE

That Mrs Delany held no position at Court may well have been part of her attraction for both the King and Queen, for they knew they could relax in her company, free from any officialdom, and yet be confident that she would never go beyond the bounds of propriety.

The Queen treated Mrs Delany like a favourite aunt and passed on to her items of domestic news. When Princess Elizabeth had whooping cough it was noted in Mrs Delany's diary, 2 December 1785; 'Princess Elizabeth very ill with inflammation on her lungs'. The entry for the next day stated that the Princess had been bled five times in forty-eight hours. At last, four weeks later, after great

Georgina Port, Mrs Delany's great-niece, whose education Mrs Delany supervised and whom she brought out into society.

166

anxiety, the Queen wrote a personal letter informing her: 'dear suffering Elizabeth has had altogether about ten hours very comfortable sleep. Her spasms still continue, but I flatter myself that the intervals are longer.' Two weeks later Georgina in a letter to her mother indicates that medicines were still being given: 'the poor little princess *takes emiticks every day* . . . and they have their backs rubbed with musk.'

Throughout these last years Mrs Delany had her great-niece Georgina Port with her almost continually. Georgina was a silver lining in Mrs Delany's life, delighting her aunt with her light-hearted chatter. As Mrs Delany's sight became increasingly limited, Georgina wrote letters which her aunt dictated, and read books, newspapers and letters to her. Georgina was about thirteen years old when they moved to Windsor, where she shared her aunt's interesting life, including entertaining the Princes and Princesses to musical evenings and games of commerce.

Another protégée of Mrs Delany was Fanny Burney, who had caused a stir in society by publishing two books in an age when it was virtually unheard of for women to do so. She stayed with Mrs Delany in London during the sad period after the Duchess of Portland's death, and consoled Mrs Delany with her company and attentions. Mrs Delany wrote:

I have had in the house with me . . . Miss Burney (the Author of Evelina and Cecilia), which excellent as they are are her meanest praise. Her admirable understanding, tender affection, and sweetness of manners, make her valuable to all those who have the happiness to know her.

Mrs Delany was also fond of Fanny's father, Dr Charles Burney, and had hoped he might fill the vacancy of Master of the Queen's Band. In the event this did not come about, and it occurred to her that it might alleviate Dr Burney's disappointment if his daughter was appointed Assistant Dresser to the Queen. Mrs Delany therefore recommended Fanny to Queen Charlotte and tried to prepare her for the new role:

I do beg of you when the Queen or the King speaks to you, not to answer with mere monosyllables. The Queen often complains to me of the difficulty with which she can get any conversation, as she not only always has to start the subjects, but, commonly, entirely to support them: and she says there is nothing she so much loves as conversations and nothing she finds so hard to get. She is always best pleased to have the answers that are made to lead her on to further discourse.

It was not altogether a happy appointment. Fanny was rather out of her depth socially, and not very accomplished as a dresser; she

Two similar portraits thought to be of Mrs Delany attributed to Benjamin West. It is known from Mrs Delany's own letters and from the diaries of Fanny Burney that Mr West was an acquaintance. He painted extensively at Windsor in this period where he enjoyed the patronage of George III. She is seen holding one of two snuff boxes of sentimental value to her. Behind the curtain is revealed Windsor Castle and the Queen's Lodge.

used to annoy the Queen by tangling her hair in her necklace. She also had a tendency to exaggerate and to make 'mountains out of molehills' as Mrs Astley, Mrs Delany's waiting-woman, later remarked. Mrs Delany was aware of the potential interest that the hundreds of letters she kept stored in a box might hold for such an ambitious young novelist and she asked Mrs Astley to sort through and burn them. Reluctantly Mrs Astley complied, but pointed out that the letters were from 'some of the highest in the land, and were worth a fortune if published'. 'That is just what I wish to avoid,' Mrs Delany replied. Although she was wary of trusting Fanny's discretion, Mrs Delany became fond of her and enjoyed her company. Fanny in return had a genuine regard for Mrs Delany and in later life was to make much of their friendship.

Although Mrs Delany spent most of her last years at Windsor, she paid occasional visits to her house at St James's Place and also sometimes went to Kew to be near the King and Queen when they stayed at the Royal Lodge. On Christmas Day 1786 she wrote:

The Royal Family once a fortnight take Kew in their way to London. They leave Windsor on Tuesday and return on Saturday. Their Majesties were so gracious as to hint their wish for my spending some days at Kew when they were there, and to make it completely commodious, engaged Mr and Mrs Smelt, who live there, to invite me to *their house* – a pleasure of *itself* that would have given me wings for the undertaking. I availed myself of the command of the one, and the invitation of the other, and spent part of two weeks there.

The house, which was beside the Thames, was only a short walk from the Royal Lodge, where Mrs Delany and the Smelts dined each day at Fanny Burney's table, before spending the remainder of the evening with the Queen in her apartment.

It was after a visit to Kew in March 1788 that Mrs Delany caught a severe chill which developed into pneumonia and on 7 April Georgina was worried about her aunt's fever and breathing difficulties. Mrs Delany was bled and blistered, bark was applied to reduce the fever, and on 13 April the doctor announced to a relieved family: 'I have reason to believe now that we shall have our old friend restored to us.' But it proved to be only a temporary respite, and her condition began to deteriorate rapidly. Finally, on 15 April, after hours of laboured breathing, Mrs Delany died. Georgina was grief-stricken at the loss of 'my – best – my – dearest friend, in my ever-blessed, ever-regretted Aunt Delany'. To Mrs Francis Hamilton in Ireland she wrote: 'Oh madam, she is no more! On

Tuesday 15th, she expired at 11 o'clock at night . . . were it not for the assurance I have of her felicity, I think it would not be possible for me to exist.'

In accordance with her will, that as little expense should be incurred in her burial as decency would permit, she was interred in a vault in her parish church of St James's Piccadilly. On the north wall there is a tablet to her memory, written by Dr Hurd:

NEAR THIS PLACE, LIE THE REMAINS OF

MARY DELANY

DAUGHTER OF BERNARD GRANVILLE

AND NIECE OF GEORGE GRANVILLE, LORD LANSDOWNE

SHE WAS MARRIED, 1ST TO ALEXANDER PENDARVES, OF ROSCROW,

IN THE COUNTY OF CORNWALL, ESQ;

AND 2ND, TO PATRICK DELANY, D.D. DEAN OF DOWN, IN IRELAND

SHE WAS BORN MAY 14, 1700 AND DIED APRIL 15, 1788

SHE WAS A LADY OF SINGULAR INGENUITY AND POLITENESS, AND OF UNAFFECTED PIETY. THESE QUALITIES ENDEARED HER THROUGH LIFE TO MANY NOBLE AND EXCELLENT PERSONS, AND MADE THE CLOSE OF IT ILLUSTRIOUS BY PROCURING FOR HER MANY SIGNAL MARKS OF GRACE AND FAVOUR FROM THEIR MAJESTIES

Of the three portraits of her painted by John Opie, one hangs at Windsor Castle, and was painted by command of George III for Queen Charlotte's bedchamber where it hung at Buckingham House, as the Palace was then known. A second was painted for the Countess of Bute and placed in a frame designed by Horace Walpole. This was elaborately carved, and the principal ornaments were intended to be emblematic of her particular accomplishments: at the top are a group of musical instruments, interspersed with sprays of bay and laurel, and at the bottom a palette forms the centre, with a miniature easel, pencils and brushes; framed by the palette is Walpole's own epitaph for Mary Delany, in which he paid tribute to her 'Piety and virtues, her excellent understanding, and her talents and taste in music and painting'. The third portrait is now in a private collection.

The one quality which could be said to represent most closely Mrs Delany's character was contentment; this was a virtue which she encouraged to grow in her own life by continually being thankful for the love of her relatives and friends, and for the beauties of nature. For an epitaph we need to go no further than quote her own words to her niece Mary Port, written in September 1780:

How thankful ought we to be for the many blessings we enjoy which no body, no accident in life, can rob us of; the reflection of *doing our duty*, the wonders and beauties of the creation, the love of our real friends as long as we are permitted the enjoyment of their *society*; and when it is the will of heaven *that* should cease, the considerations that all tryals are sent to refine us for a blessed state, where only true (that is permanent) joys are to be found.

The 142 steps leading up to Hanbury Church, Worcestershire, a drawing by Mrs Delany.

Collages by Mrs Delany in the British Museum

This list is compiled from the inscriptions in Mrs Delany's own hand on the reverse of her near-1000 collages kept in volumes in the British Museum. Her inconsistencies of spelling, punctuation and abbreviation have been retained. Where common names are not inscribed on the collages, the author has added those from Mrs Delany's own *Index* to the volumes. 'Prov[enence]' has been added to indicate the difference, if any, between where the collage was created and where the plant was grown.

Key

Line 1: Mrs Delany's number; Latin name; common name; British Museum reference number

Line 2: The Linnaean classification given by Mrs Delany

Line 3: Place and date of composition (where known)

Line 4: Donor of plant, or where it was grown (where known)

British Museum reference numbers are in italics and are prefixed by 1897–5–5.

Volume I

1 *Acanthus Spinosus* Bear's Breech *1*
Dydinamia Angospermia
Bulstrode 8.6.78

2 *Achillea Alpina* Alpine Milfoil *2*
Syngenesia Polygamia Superfl
Bulstrode 5.9.76

3 *Achillea Millefolium* Common Yarrow *3*
Syngenesia Polygamia Superfl
Bulstrode 27.11.76

4 *Aconitum Napellus* Wolf's Bane or Monkshood *4*
Polyandria Trygynia
Bulstrode 1774

5 *Adonis Annua Autumnulis* Pheasant's Eye *5*
Polyandria Polygynia
Bulstrode 20.9.76

6 *Adoxa Moschatellina* Tuberous Moschatel *6*
St James's Place, 6.5.80
Prov: Bulstrode

7 *Aeschelus Hippocastanum* Horse Chestnut *7*
Heptandria Monogynia
Bulstrode 6.6.76

8 *Agrostemma Flos Jovis* Jove's Campion *8*

9 *Agrostemma Githago* Corn Cockle *9*
Duandria Pentagynia
Bulstrode 3.7.79

10 *Albuca Major* Bastard star of Bethlem *10*
Hexandria Monogynia
Luton 15.8.77

11 *Alcea Rosea* Chinese Hollyhock *11*
Monodelphia Polyd
Bulstrode 23.7.79

12 *Aletris Capensis 12*
Hexdria Mon
St James's Place 3.80
Prov: Bulstrode

13 *Aletris Iris Uvaria 13*
Hexandria Mono
St James's Place 19.8.79
Prov: Mr Lee.

14 *Allium Arenarium* Mountain Garlick *14*
Bulstrode 17.7.80

15 *Allium Moly* Homer's Moly, a garlic *15*
Hexandria Monogynia
Bulstrode 15.6.79

16 *Allium Inodorum* Scentless Garlick *16*
St James's Place 28.5.81
Prov: Kew

17 *Allium Ampeloprasum* Holm's Garlick *17*
Bulstrode 8.8.81

18 *Aloe Perfoliata*. var Tree Aloe *18*
St James's Place 5.10.80
Prov. Chelsea Physic Garden

19 *Aloe Perfoliata* var *19*
Hexandria Monogynia
St James's Place 9.3.76

20 *Alstromeria Ligtu 20*
Hexandria Monogynia
St James's Place 8.1.79
Prov: Mr Lee, Hammersmith

21 *Alstromeria Pilegrina* Peruvian lily *21*
Hexandria Monogynia
Bulstrode 21.6.76

22 *Alypum Longifolium Solandri 22*
Bulstrode 12.10.80
Prov: Kew

23 *Alyssum Saxatile* Rock Madwort *23*
Tetradynamia Siliculosa
St James's Place 26.5.78
Prov: Mrs Dashwood

24 *Alyssum Utriculatum* Bladder Madwort *24*
Tetra: Sili.
1779
Prov: Dr Pitcairn

25 *Amaryllis Reginae* Mexican lily Lin Sec *25*
Millers Plate XXIII described under XXIV
1775

26 *Amaryllis Belladonna* Regina Solander *26*
Hex: Monog:
Bulstrode 15.10.79
Prov: Mr Lee

27 *Amaryllis ? Attamyasco 27*
St James's Place 8.6.78
Prov: Mr Lee

28 *Amaryllis Lutea* Yellow Autumnal amaryllis *28*
Hexandria Monogynia
Bulstrode 22.10.76

29 *Amaryllis Aurea Solander 29*
Bulstrode 21.10.79
Prov: Mr Lee

30 *Amaryllis Belladonna* Lily Daffodil *30*
Hexandria Monogynia
Bulstrode 18.9.75

31 *Amaryllis Sarniensis* Guernsey Lily *31*
Hex: Mono:
Bulstrode 9.75

32 *Amaryllis Formosissima* Jacobaean Lily *32*
Hexandria Monogynia
Bulstrode 21.9.75

33 *Amaryllis Undulata* With waved leaves *33*
Hexandria Monogynia
Bulstrode 4.11.76
Prov: Kew

34 *Amaryllis Regis Solandri 34*
St James's Place 16.3.81
Prov: Queen Charlotte

35 *Amaryllis Spatha Uniflora 35*
St James's Place 26.4.81
Prov: Dr Pitcairn

36 *Amaranthus Tricolor 36*
Bulstrode 9.8.81

37 *Ammi Majus* Bishop's Weed *37*
Polyandria Dygenia
Bulstrode 2.11.78

38 *Amygdalus Nana* Dwarf almond *38*
St James's Place 1.5.78
Prov: Ld Willoughby's Marsh garden

39 *Amygdalus Communis* Almond *39*
Icosandria Monogynia
St James's Place 1775

40 *Amygdalus Persica* Double flowering peach *40*
St James's Place 25.4.78
Prov: Mrs Astley, Barnes

41 *Anagallis Arvensis* Scarlet Pimpernel *41*
Pentandria Monogynia
Bulstrode 7.10.76

42 *Anagallis Monelli* Monellus's Blue Pimpernel *42*
Pentandria Monogynia
Bulstrode 12.6.76

43 *Anagallis Tinella* Purple Moneywort *43*
Pentandria Monogynia
Bulstrode 24.7.77

44 *Andromeda Dabaecia* Irish Heath *44*
Decandria Monogynia
Bulstrode 1774

45 *Andromeda Polifolia* Rosemary leaved *45*
Bulstrode 30.9.76

46 *Andromeda Polifolia* var Americana *46*
St James's Place 6.5.78
Prov: Islington [Dr Pitcairn]

47 *Andromeda* from North America *47*
Decandria Monogynia
Bulstrode 25.6.76

48 *Andryala Lanata 48*
Syngen: Polyg: Aqual:
Bulstrode 30.10.78

49 *Anemone Hortensis* Garden Anemone *49*
St James's Place 7.4.79
Prov: Mr B. Grey from Dr Fothergill's [garden]
    Upton, Essex

50 *Anemone Hepatica* var *50*
St James's Place 25.3.78

51 *Anemone Virginiana 51*
Polyandria Polygynia
Bulstrode 1.6.76

52 *Anemone Pulsatilla* Pasque Flower *52*
St James's Place 28.4.80
Prov: Bulstrode

53 *Anemone Pulsatilla* Pasque Flower *53*
St James's Place 8.5.80
Prov: Bulstrode

54 *Anemone Apennina* Mountain blue *54*
Polyandria Polygynia
St James's Place 26.3.76

55 *Anemone Nemorosa* Wood Anemone *55*
Polyandria Polygynia
St James's Place 27.3.76

56 *Annona Isopetala* Custard Apple *56*
Polyandria Polygynia
Bulstrode 5.9.77
Prov: Sion House

57 *Annona Triloba* Hardy Papaw *57*
5.75
Prov: Bulstrode

58 *Anthemis Valentina* Italian Chamomile *58*
Singenesia Poly: Superfl:
Bulstrode 12.10.78
Prov: Mr Yalden

59 *Anthemis Arvensis* Field Camomile *59*
Singenesia Polyg Superfl
Bulstrode 10.11.79

60 *Anthemis Tinctoria* Oxe eye Camomile *60*
Bulstrode 15.7.80

61 *Anthericum Frutiscens* Yellow sedum *61*
Hexandria Monogynia
Bulstrode 19.7.77

62 *Anthericum Liliago* Spiderwort *62*
Hexandria Monogynia
Bulstrode 1774

63 *Anthericum Revolutum 63*
Hexandria Monogynia
Bulstrode 11.77
Prov: Kew

64 *Antholiza Cunonia 70*
Tryandria Monogynia
St James's Place 15.4.79
Prov: Dr. Fothergill, Upton, Essex

65 *Antholiza Meriana 71*
Triandria Monogynia
Luton 6.78

66 *Antirrhinum Genistifolium* Broom Snapdragon *72*
Dydinamia Angiospermia
Bulstrode 2.10.79
Prov: Kew

67 *Antirrhinum Spurium* Round-Fluellin *73*
Bulstrode 23.9.79

68 *Antirrhinum Elatine* Angular Fluellin *74*

69 *Antirrhinum Majus* var Crimson Snapdragon *75*
Bulstrode 2.7.78
Prov: Ld Bute, Luton

70 *Antirrhinum Linaria* Yellow toad flax *76*
Didygamia Angiosperma
Bulstrode 14.9.76

71 *Antirrhinum Tryphyllum* Ternate Snapdragon *77*
Dydinamia Angiosperma
Bulstrode 3.10.76

72 *Antirrhinum Repens* Henley Toad-flax *78*
Dydinamia Gymnosp:
Bulstrode 29.9.77

73 *Antirrhinum Cymbalaria* Ivy Leav'd toad flax *79*
Didynamia Angiosperma
Bulstrode 17.9.76

74 *Apocynum Androsamifolium* Catch-fly Dog's bane
    80
Pentandria Dyginia
Bulstrode 18.7.78

75 *Arctotis Aspera 81*
St James's Place 17.4.79
Prov: Dr Fothergill, Upton, Essex

76 *Arctotis Paleacia 82*
Syngensia Polygamia Necessaria
St James's Place 29.5.79
Prov: Mr Lee

77 *Arctotis Calendulacea* Marigold-like Arctotis *83*
Syng: Poly: Necessaria
St James's Place 27.5.77
Prov: Dr Pitcairn, Islington

78 *Arduina Bispinosa* Bastard Lycium *84*
[?] Monogynia
Bulstrode 28.7.78
Prov: Chelsea Physic Garden

79 *Arbutus Andrachne* Easter Strawberry Tree *85*
St James's Place 31.3.79
Prov: Kew

80 *Arbutus Unedo* White flowering *86*
Decandria Monogynia
Bulstrode 27.11.75

81 *Arbutus Unedo* var Red flowering arbutus *87*
Decandria Monogynia
Bulstrode 11.76

82 *Arbutus Uva Ursi* Bear berries *88*
St James's Place 21.3.76

83 *Aristolochia Pistolochia* Trailing Birthwort *89*
Gyandria Hexandria
Bulstrode 4.7.78
Prov: Luton, Ld Bute

84 *Aristolochia Rotunda* Round Birthwort *90*
St James's Place 18.5.81
Prov: *Kew*

85 *Aristolochia Macrophylla*, Solandri Birthwort *91*
Gynandria Hexandria
St James's Place 31.5.79
Bulstrode

86 *Arum Pictum* New sp: of Solander *92*
Gynandria Polyandria
St James's Place 8.6.78 & 31.7.80
Prov: Mr Lee

87 *Arum Divaricatum* Wake Robin or Fryers Coin
    93
Bulstrode 29.10.79

88 *Arum Tenuifolium* Narrow leav'd *94*
Gynandria Polyandria
Bulstrode 26.7.76

89 *Arum Esculentum* Eatable Wake-Robin *95*
St James's Place 3.80
From a drawing by Lady Ann Monson, Madras

90 *Asclepias Gigantea* Great Swallow-wort *96*
Pentandria Digynia
Bulstrode 8.7.76

91 *Asclepias Curasavica* Swallow-wort *97*
Pentandria Dygynia
St James's Place 16.8.79
Prov: Mr Lee

54 *Campanula Patula* wide spreading Bell-flower *155*
Pentandria Monogynia
Bulstrode 16.7.76

55 *Canarina Campanula* Canary Bellflower *156*
Tentandria Monogynia
Bulstrode 1774

56 *Canna Indica* Indian Reed *157*
Monandria Monogynia
Bulstrode 20.6.76

57 *Cardamine Pratensis* Common ladies smock *158*
St James's Place 9.5.80

58 *Carduus Lanceolatus* Spear thistle *159*
Syngenesia Polygamia Equalis
Bulstrode 19.11.76

59 *Carduus Marianus* Milk Thistle *160*
Syng. Poly. Aqualis
Bulstrode 1.11.78

60 *Carduus Nutans* Musk or Nodding thistle *161*
Syngenesia Polygandria Aequalis
Bulstrode 26.11.76

61 *Carduus Acaulis* Dwarf carline thistle *162*
Bulstrode 30.9.79

62 *Carduus Eriophorus* Cotton-headed thistle *163*
Bulstrode 4.8.81

63 *Carthamus Tinctorius* Scarlet Saff flower *164*
Bulstrode 7.10.79
Prov: Miss Jennings

64 *Carthamus Caruleus* Purple saff *165*
Sygens: Polygam: Aqualis
Bulstrode 16.10.77

65 *Cassia Marylandica 166*
Bulstrode 23.9.78
Prov: Lord Mansfield

66 *Cassine Maurocenia* var: Hottentot-Cherry *167*
Pentand: Trygyn:
Bulstrode 30.10.78

67 *Catesbaea Spinosa* Lily-thorn *168*
Bulstrode 4.9.80

68 *Caucalis Grandiflora* Bastard Parsley *169*
Pentan; Digynia
Bulstrode 3.11.78
Prov: Mr Yalden

69 *Caucalis Latifolia* Broad leav'd Parsley *170*
Bulstrode 7.7.78

70 *Ceonothus Africanus 171*
St James's Place 9.4.79
Prov: Mr B. Grey

71 *Celastrus Pyracanthus* African Barbery *172*
Octandria Monogynia
Bulstrode 17.11.77

72 *Celsia Arcturus* Bastard Mullein *173*
Bulstrode 15.10.78
Prov: Mr Yalden

73 *Centaurea Peregrina* Great Centaurea *174*
St James's Place 1.9.78
Prov: Dr Pitcairn

74 *Centaurea Seridis 175*
Bulstrode 16.10.78

75 *Centaurea Melitensis* Malta Thistle *176*
Synegesia Polygamia frustrania
Bulstrode 6.9.76

76 *Centaurea Amberboi* Yellow sultan *177*
Syngenes Polygam. frust.
Bulstrode 11.11.77

77 *Centaurea Alpina* Great Yellow Sultan *178*
Syngenesia Polygamia frust.
Bulstrode 28.6.77

78 *Centaurea Moschata* Sweet sultan *179*
Bulstrode 10.77

79 *Centaurea Cyanus* Blue bottle *180*
Bulstrode 25.6.79

80 *Centunculus Minimus 181*
Bulstrode 24.7.78

81 *Cerastium Aquaticum* Great Water-chickweed *182*
Bulstrode 19.10.80

82 *Cheiranthus Cheiri* Bloody wall flower *183*
St James's Place 2.5.78
Prov: Mrs Boscawen, Glanvilla

83 *Cheiranthus Sinuatus* Sea Gilliflower *184*
Tetradynamia Seliquosa
Bulstrode 6.75

84 *Cheiranthus Annuus* Dwarf annual stock gilliflower *185*
Tetradynamia Seliquosa
Bulstrode 23.11.76

85 *Cheiranthus Incanus* Double Stock *186*
St James's Place 8.5.79
Prov: Blackheath

86 *Chelidonium Glaucium* Yellow horned poppy *187*
Bulstrode 7.80

87 *Chelone Glabra 188*
Bulstrode 27.9.80

88 *Chironia Frutescens 189*
Pentandria Monogynia
Bulstrode 30.10.77
Prov: Kew

89 *Chlora Perfoliata* Yellow centory *190*
Octandria Monogynia
Bulstrode 12.7.77

90 *Chrysanthemum Lucanthemum* Common Ox eye daisy *191*
Syngensia Polyg: Super:
Bulstrode 1774

91 *Chrysocoma Comaurea* Great African Goldy Locks *192*
Bulstrode 18.9.79

92 *Chrysosplenium Oppositifol* Opposite Golden saxifrage *193*
St James's Place 10.5.80
Prov: Bulstrode

93 *Cichorium Intybus* Wild Succory *194*
Syngenesia Polygamia Aequalis
Bulstrode 23.9.76

94 *Cineraria Populifolia*, Poplar-leav'd Ashweed *195*
St James's Place 6.6.81
Prov: Kew

95 *Cineraria Amelloides* African bastard starwort *196*
Syngen: Polygam: Superfl:
Bulstrode 13.7.78

96 *Cineraria Geifolia 197*
Syngenes: Polygam:
Bulstrode 14.10.77
Prov: Kew

97 *Circea Alpina* Enchanter's Nightshade *198*
Bulstrode 29.7.79

98 *Circae* Enchanter's Nightshade *199*
Decandria Monogynia
Bulstrode 18.7.77

99 *Cestrum Nocturnum 200*
Pentandria Monogynia
Bulstrode 17.11.75

100 *Cistus Surreianus* Surry dwarf sunflower *201*
Bulstrode 22.7.78

Volume III

1 *Cistus Helianthemum 202*
Polyandria Monogynia
Bulstrode 10.9.77
Prov: Kew

2 *Cistus Helianthemum* Dwarf sunflower *203*
Bulstrode 18.6.79

3 *Cistus Laxus* Loose rock-rose *204*
Bulstrode 25.8.81

4 *Cistus Formosus 205*
Polyandria Monogynia
Luton 6.78

5 *Citrus Medica* Double flower'd citron *206*
Polyandria Icosandria
Bulstrode 8.7.78

6 *Claytonia Media* New species *207*
St James's Place 27.3.78
Prov: Dr Pitcairn

7 *Clematis Vitalba* Traveller's Joy *208*
Polyandria Monogynia
Bulstrode 3.8.76

8 *Clematis Flammula* Sweet Virgin's Bower *209*
Polyandria Polygynia
Bulstrode 1.11.77
Prov: Kew

9 *Clematis Crispa* Crisped Virgin's Bower *210*
Polyandria Polygynia
Bulstrode 2.9.76

10 *Clematis Orientalis* Oriental Virgin's Bower *211*
Bulstrode 31.8.80
Prov: Kew

11 *Cleome Pentaphylla 212*
Tetradinamia Siliquosa
Luton 16.8.77

12 *Cleome Gigantea 213*
Bulstrode 19.9.78

13 *Clethra Alnifolia* Virginian Cat's-tail *214*
Bill Hill 1.9.79

14 *Clitoria Ternataea 215*
Diadelphia Decand:
Bulstrode 6.7.78

15 *Clutia Pulchella 216*
Bulstrode 2.11.79

16 *Clypeola Maritima 217*
Tetragynia Siliculos

17 *Cneorum Tricoccum* Widow-wail *218*
St James's Place 29.4.80

18 *Coix Lacrymajobi* Job's Tears *219*
Bulstrode 2.11.80

19 *Colchicum Autumnale* Meadow Saffron *220*
Bulstrode 26.9.76

20 *Commelina Africana 221*
Lin 3-d i-9
Bulstrode 14.9.80

21 *Columnea* of Brown's History of Jamaica *222*
Didynamia Angiosperma
St James's Place 10.9.78
Prov: Chelsea Physic Garden

22 *Coniza Linifolia* Fleabane *223*
Syngenesia Polygamia Superfl:
Bulstrode 4.7.78

23 *Convallaria Majalis* Lilly of the valley *224*
Hexandria Monogynia
St James's Place 8.5.76

24 *Convallaria Majalis* with double flowers *225*
St James's Place 22.4.78
Prov: Bulstrode

25 *Convolvulus Sapium* Giant bindweed *226*
Pentandria Monogynia
Bulstrode 29.7.76

26 *Convolvulus* non-descript *227*
Pentandria Monogynia
Bulstrode 1.7.78
Prov: Luton

27 *Convolvulus Arvensis* Field Bindweed *228*
Pentandria Monogynia
St James's Place 8. [?]

28 *Coronilla Varia* Reclining coronilla *229*
Diadelphia Decandria
Bulstrode 15.11.76

29 *Coronilla Glauca* with sea green leaves *230*
Diadelphia decandria
Bulstrode 12.11.76

30 *Coronilla Emerus* Scorpion senna *231*
Bulstrode 11.11.79

31 *Coronilla Cretica 232*
Bulstrode 17.10.78

32 *Cornus Mascula* Cornelian Cherry *233*
St James's Place 3.4.78
Prov: Bulstrode

33 *Cornus Canadensis 234*
St James's Place 14.5.79
Prov: Kew

34 *Cotyledon Umbilicus* Navel wort *235*
Bulstrode 12.6.79

35 *Cotyledon Orbiculata* Round leav'd *236*
Decandria Pentagynia
Bulstrode 8.8.76

36 *Cucubalus Bacciferus* Berry-bearing chickweed *237*
Bulstrode 20.7.78

37 *Cucubalus Behen* Bladder campion *238*
Bulstrode 13.7.80

38 *Cucubalus Tartaricus* Tartarian Campion *239*
St James's Place 18.7.81
Prov: Kew, Mr Farwell

39 *Curcuma Longa* Turmerick *240*
Monandria Monogynia
Luton 18.8.77

40 *Crassula Scabra* Rough Orpine *241*
Bulstrode 10.78

41 *Crassula* non-descript *242*
Pentandria Pentagynia
Bulstrode 13.9.77
Prov: Kew

42 *Crassula Coccinea 243*
Pentandria Pentagynia
Bulstrode 4.10.77
Prov: Luton

43 *Crasula Laciniata 244*
Pentandria Pentagynia
St James's Place 23.5.78
Prov: Blackheath, Lord Dartmouth

44 *Crassula* non-descript *245*
Bulstrode 23.10.81

45 *Crataegus Oxyacantha* Hawthorn *246*
Icosandria Digynia
Bulstrode 6.76

46 *Cratagus Aria* The White Beam tree *247*
Icosandria Dygynia
St James's Place 29.5.76

47 *Crinum Zeylanicum* Asphodil Lilly *248*
Hexandria Monogynia
St James's Place 14.4.78
Prov: Lord Rockingham

48 *Crinum Africanum* Blue African Crinum *249*
Hexandria Monogynia
Luton 20.8.76

49 *Crinum Asiaticum* Asiatic Crinum *250*
St James's Place 12.5.80
Prov: Mr Lee, Hammersmith

50 *Crocus Sativus Officinal* saffron *251*
Triandria Monogynia
Bulstrode 15.10.76

51 *Crocus Vernus* A striped variety *252*
St James's Place 14.3.76

52 *Crocus Vernus* the yellow kind *253*
Triandria Monogynia
St James's Place 2.76

53 *Crotalaria Retusa 254*
Bulstrode 20.10.79
Prov: Mr Lee

54 *Crotalaria Laburnifolia* Yellow asiatick *255*
Diadelphia Decandria
Bulstrode 17.7.76

55 *Cyclamen Europaeum* Sow bread *256*
Pentandria Monogynia
Bulstrode 10.1.77

56 *Cynanchum Acutum 257*
Bulstrode 7.9.76[?]

57 *Cynanchium* the Species unknown *258*
Pentandria Digynia
Bulstrode 3.7.78
Prov: Luton

58 *Cynanchium Extensum Solandri 259*
Bulstrode 20.9.79
Prov: Kew

59 *Cynoglossum Omphalodes* Hounds tongue *260*
Pentandria Monogynia
St James's Place 1.4.76

60 *Cypripedium Purpureum* American Lady's Slipper *261*
Gynandria Diandria
Bulstrode 1774

61 *Cyprepedium Calceolus* Ladies slipper *262*
Gynandria Diandria
Bulstrode 13.5.75

62 *Cytissus Glutinosus 263*
Bulstrode 22.10.79

63 *Cytisus Laburnum 264*
Diadelphia Decandria
St James's Place 15.5.76

64 *Cytisus Cajan* Pigeon Pea *265*
Bulstrode 31.7.79

65 *Daphne Cneorum* Red sweet scented *266*
Tetrandia Monogynia
Bulstrode 5.9.76

66 *Daphne Flaveolens* New sp Solander from ye East indies *267*
Octandria Monogynia
Prov: Bulstrode 30.3.78

67 *Daphne Mezereon* Mezerion tree *268*
Octandria Monogynia
St James's Place 28.3.78

68 *Daphne Laureola* Spurge laurel *269*
Octandria Monogynia
St James's Place 3.4.78

69 *Delphinium Staphisagria* Staves acre *270*
Polyandria Trigynia
St James's Place 22.4.77
Prov: Kew

70 *Delphinium Consolida* Common larkspur *271*
Polyandria Trigynia
Bulstrode 10.76

71 *Dentaria Bulbifera* Coral wort *272*
Tetradynamia Seliquosa
Bulstrode 5.75

72 *Dianthus Armeria* Deptford Pink *273*
Bulstrode 5.7.80

73 *Dianthus Superbus* Feather'd Pink *274*
Bulstrode 1774

74 *Dianthus Caryophyllus* Pheasant Ey'd pink *275*
Decandria Digynia
Bulstrode 23.7.77

75 *Dianthus Caryophyllus* 2 varieties *276*
St James's Place 3.6.78
Prov: Mrs Dashwood

76 *Dianthus Caryophyllus* Pink or Carnation var: *277*
Bulstrode 17.8.78
Prov: The Queen [Charlotte]

77 *Dianthus Caryophyllus* Jersey pink *278*
St James's Place 8.9.79
Prov: General Conway, Park Place, [originally] from Jersey

78 *Dianthus Deltoides* Maiden pink *279*
Bulstrode 9.8.80

79 *Dianthus Arenarius* Cheddar Pink *280*
Bulstrode 15.6.79

80 *Dictamnus albus* Fraxinella *281*
Decandria Monogynia
Bulstrode 17.7.76

81 *Digitalis Purpurea* Purple fox glove *282*
Bulstrode 21.7.76

82 *Digitalis Canariensis* Canary fox glove *283*
Didynamia Angiospermia
Bulstrode 6.8.77
Prov: Luton

83 *Digitalis Erubescens* Blush foxglove *284*

84 *Diosma Lanceolata* Lance leav'd Diosma *285*
Pentandria Monogynia
St James's Place 14.5.79
Prov: Kew

85 *Diosma Ericoides 286*

86 *Diosma Hirsuta* Hairy diosma *287*

87 *Diosma Oppositifolia* Opposite leav'd Diosma
288
Bulstrode 28.9.80

88 *Disa Aulica, Solandri 289*
St James's Place 4.2.80
From a drawing of Lady Anne Monson

89 *Disandra Prostrata 290*
Heptandria Monogynia
Bulstrode 22.10.77

90 *Dodecatheon Meadia 291*
Pentandria Monogynia
Bulstrode 5.75

91 *Dolichos Purpurea? 292*
St James's Place 25.5.81
Prov: Kew

92 *Dolichos Lablab 293*
Diadelphia Decandria
Bulstrode 18.9.78

93 *Draba Aizoides 294*
St James's Place 27.3.78
Prov: Dr Pitcairn Islington

94 *Draba Incana* Writhen podded Whitlow grass
295
Bulstrode 18.6.79

95 *Dracocephalum Moldavica* Moldavian Balm *296*
Bulstrode 21.9.80

96 *Dracana Terminalis* Purple Dragon-tree *297*
St James's Place 4.80
Prov: Dr Pitcairn, Islington

97 *Drosera Rotundifolia* Sundew *298*
Bulstrode 27.7.80

98 *Echinops Ritro* Lesser Globe Thistle *299*
Bulstrode 9.8.79

99 *Echium Vulgare* Vipers Bugloss *300*
Pentandria Monogynia
Bulstrode 7.7.77

100 *Epimedium Alpinum* Barren-wort *301*
Tetrandria Monogynia
Bulstrode 5.75

Volume IV

1 *Epilobium Ramosum* Codlings and cream *302*
Bulstrode 10.8.81

2 *Epilobium Gelidum* Willowherb Solander *303*
St James's Place 2.9.78
Prov: Dr Pitcairn

3 *Erica Cerinthoides* Ethiopia *304*
Octandria Monogynia
Luton 29.8.77

4 *Erica Ciliaris 305*
Octandria Monogynia

5 *Erica Cinerea* Fine leav'd heath *306*
Octandria Monogynia
Bulstrode 25.9.76

6 *Erica Multiflora* Fir leav'd heath *307*
Octandria Monogynia
Bulstrode 9.76

7 *Erica Longiflora* Long flower'd Heath *308*
Octandria Monogynia
St James's Place 1.6.79
Prov: Mr Lee

8 *Erica Tubiflora 309*
Octandria Monogynia
St James's Place 16.4.78
Prov: Dr Pitcairn, Islington

9 *Erica Longiflora (Curviflora)* Long yellow flowers
310
Octandria Monogynia
Luton Park 24.6.78

10 *Erica Grandiflora* Red and yellow flowers *311*
Bulstrode 9.9.77
Prov: Kew

11 *Erica Coccinea?* Scarlet tubular flowers *312*
Octandria Monogynia
Bulstrode 5.11.76
Prov: Kew

12 *Erica (Baccans)* from the Cape Heath *313*
Octandria Monogynia
St James's Place

13 *Erica Mediterranea* Mediterranean Heath *314*
St James's Place 7.5.[?]
Prov: Mr Lee

14 *Erica Arborea 315*
Octandria Monogynia
St James's Place 28.4.77
Prov: Kew

15 *Erigeron* New *316*
Syng. Polygam. Superfl.
Bulstrode 25.11.78
Prov: Kew

16 *Erinus Venustus 317*
Bulstrode 19.11.79
Prov: Mr Lee

17 *Eryingium Alpinum 318*
Pentandria Digynia
Bulstrode 24.6.76
Prov: Kew

18 *Erysimum Cheiranthoides* Treacle wormword *319*
Bulstrode 4.10.78

19 *Erythrina Fulgens 320*
St James's Place 3.80
From a drawing of Lady Anne Monson

20 *Erythrina Herbacea* Coral tree *321*
Diadelphia Decan:
Bulstrode 7.75

21 *Erythronium* Dogs tooth violet *322*
Hexandria Monogynia
St James's Place 10.4.78

22 *Eugenia Jambos 323*
Bulstrode 20.8.81

23 *Eugenia Oppositifolia* a new species *324*
St James's Place 24.1.80
Prov: Kew

24 *Euphrasia Officinalis* Eyebright *325*
Bulstrode 28.9.78

25 *Euphorbia Amygdoloides* variagated spurge *326*
Dodecandria Trigynia
St James's Place 28.5.77
Prov: Dr Pitcairn, Islington

26 *Euphorbia Hyberna 327*
Dodecandria Trigynia
Bulstrode 1775

27 *Euphorbia heterophylla 328*
Bulstrode 9.11.80

28 *Euonymus Europans* Spindle tree [flower] *329*
Pentandria Monogynia
Bulstrode 5.75

28 *Euonymus Europans* Spindle tree [fruit] *329**
Bulstrode 9.74

29 *Fagonia Cretica* Cretan fagonia *330*
Bulstrode 18.11.79
Prov: Mr Lee

30 *Ficus Nitida* Shining fig-tree *331*
Bulstrode 27.8.81

31 *Fothergilla of Solander 332*
St James's Place 5.6.78
Prov: Chelsea Physic Garden

32 *Fragaria Vesca* Wood strawberry *333*
Icosandria Polygn.
Bulstrode 21.6.77

33 *Fritillaria Meleagris* Chequer'd Daffodil *334*
St James's Place 13.4.78
Prov: Bulstrode

34 *Fritillaria Imperialis 335*
Hexandria Monogynia
Bulstrode 20.9.75

34 *Fritilaria Imperialis 335**

35 *Fumaria officianalis* Common Fumitory *336*
Bulstrode 1.7.79

36 *Fumaria Sempervirens* Glaucus Fumitory *337*
9.6.79

37 *Fumaria Fungosa* new species Climbing fumitory
338
Diadelphia hexandria
Bill Hill 23.8.76
Prov: Luton Park

38 *Fumaria Vesicaria* Ethiopian fumitory *339*
Diadelphia Hexandria
Luton Park 21.6.78

39 *Fumaria Lutea* Yellow fumitory *340*
Diadelphia Hexandria
Bulstrode 4.11.77

40 *Galega Rosea* New species *341*
Diadelphia Decandria
Bulstrode 29.10.77
Prov: Kew

41 *Galega Officinalis* Goat's Rue *342*
Bulstrode 31.8.81

42 *Galeopsis Tetrahit* Nettle Hemp *343*
Didynamia Gymnospermia
Bulstrode 16.7.77

43 *Galeopsis Villosa* Yellow Yorkshire Ironwort *344*
Bulstrode 2.8.79

44 *Galanthus Nivalis* Single snowdrop *345*
St James's Place 28.2.77

45 *Galanthus Nivalis* Double snowdrop *346*
St James's Place 4.75

46 *Galium Borcale* Mountain bedstraw *347*
Bulstrode 20.7.80

47 *Gardenia Florida* double Cape Jessamine *348*
Pentandria Monogynia
Bulstrode 1.9.77

48 *Gardenia Florida* Single Cape Jessamine *349*
Bulstrode 29.6.79

49 *Gaura Biennis 350*
Octandria Monogynia
12.6.77
Prov: Bulstrode

50 *Genista Virgata* Long twig'd genista *351*
Bulstrode 30.11.79
Prov: Mr Lee

51 *Genista Alba, Solandri 352*
St James's Place 17.5.79
Prov: Kew

52 *Genista Canariensis* Canary Broom *353*
Diadelphia Decandria
Bulstrode 16.11.76

53 *Gentiana Pneumonanthe* Calathian gentian *354*
Bulstrode 18.9.80

54 *Gentiana Amarella* Autumnal gentian *355*
Bulstrode 1780

55 *Gentiana Imperialis* Imperial gentian *356*
Bulstrode 9.8.80

56 *Gentiana Asclepiadea 357*
Bulstrode 5.10.78

57 *Gentiana Centaurium* or Lesser Centary *358*
Syngensia Poly. Frust.
Bulstrode 1774

58 *Geranium Sanguineum* Bloody cranesbill *359*

59 *Geranium Sanguineum Flore Striate* Lancashire
  Cranesbill *359**

60 *Geranium Rotundifolium* Round leav'd cranesbill
  360
Monodelphia Decandria
Bulstrode 31.10.76

61 *Geranium Robertianum* Herb Robert *361*
Bulstrode 21.6.79

62 *Geranium Pyrenaicum* Perennial Cranesbill *362*
Bulstrode 1780

63 *Geranium Lucidum* Shining Cranesbill *363*
Bulstrode 7.7.80

64 *Geranium Pratense* Crowfoot Cranesbill *364*
Bulstrode 6.7.80

65 *Geranium Sylvaticum* Wood Cranesbill *365*
Bulstrode 16.6.79

66 *Geranium Nodosum* Knotty geranium *366*
Bulstrode 1780

67 *Geranium Myrrhifolium 367*
Monodelphia Decand.
Bulstrode 1774

68 *Geranium Odoratissimum* Allspice Geranium *368*
Monodelphia Decandria
Bulstrode 24.10.77

69 *Geranium Hermanifolium* Hermania-leav'd
  geranium *369*
Monodelphia Decandria
St James's Place 16.4.77
Prov: Kew

70 *Geranium Papilionaceum 370*
Monodelphia Decandria
St James's Place 18.4.78

71 *Geranium Peltatum 371*
Bulstrode 20.10.78
Prov: Sir George Howard

72 *Geranium Inquinans 372*
Bulstrode 21.10.78
Prov: Sir George Howard

73 *Geranium Radula* of Solander new species *373*
Monodelphia Decandria
St James's Place 10.6.78
Prov: Bulstrode

74 *Geranium Lacerum* new species Solandri *374*
Monodelphia Decandria
Bulstrode 19.11.78
Prov: Kew

75 *Geranium Lanceolatum, Solandri 375*
Monodelphia Decandria
St James's Place 12.8.77
Prov: Mr Lee

76 *Geranium Lobatum* Vine-leav'd geranium *376*
Bulstrode 6.9.80

77 *Geranium Macrorhizon* Long rooted geranium
  377
Monodelphia Decandria
Bulstrode 1773

78 *Geranium Scabrum*, Rough geranium *378*
Bulstrode 19.10.79
Prov: Mr Lee

79 *Geranium Striatum* Vein'd geranium *379*
Monodelphia Decandria
Bulstrode 22.6.76

80 *Geranium Gruinum 380*
Monodelphia Decandria
Bulstrode 11.6.77

81 *Geranium* African terebinthinum, *381*
Monodelphia Decandria
Bulstrode 11.12.76
Prov: Kew

82 *Geranium Trigonum* From ye Cape Solander
  new species *382*
Bulstrode 30.10.78
Prov: Kew

83 *Geranium Triste* Night-smelling geranium *383*
St James's Place 13.8.79
Prov: Chelsea Physic Garden

84 *Geranium Zonale 384*
Bulstrode 20.10.78

85 *Geranium Zonale* var *385*
Monodelphia Decandria
Bulstrode 7.78

86 *Geranium* Dwarf geranium Reichardi *386*
Monodelphia Decandria
Bulstrode 9.9.76

87 *Geranium Cucullatum 387*
Monodelphia Decandria
Bulstrode 1774

88 *Geranium Capitatum 388*
Monodelphia Decandria
Bulstrode 23.10.76

89 *Geranium Alchemilloides 389*
Bulstrode 19.10.78
Prov: Sir George Howard

90 *Geranium Acetosum* Sorrel leav'd geranium *390*
Monodelphia Decandria
Luton 26.8.77

91 *Geranium Fulgidum* Scarlet geranium *391*
Monodelphia Decandria
Bulstrode 7.75

92 *Geranium Lavigatum Solandri 392*
St James's Place 6.7.81
Prov: Kew

93 *Geranium Gibbosum* Gouty geranium *393*
Bill Hill 4.9.79
Prov: Miss Jennings, Shiplack

94 *Gesnera Tomentosa 394*
St James's Place 8.4.79
Prov: Dr Fothergill, Upton Essex

95 *Gladiolus Plicatus* Pleated-leav'd Corn-flag *395*
Triandria Monogynia
St James's Place 18.5.[?]

96 *Gloriosa Superba 396*
Hexandria Monogynia
Bulstrode 19.9.[?]

97 *Gnaphalium Ericoides 397*
Syng: Polyg: Superfl:
St James's Place 1.4.78
Prov: Dr Pitcairn, Islington

98 *Gordonia Lasianthus* Loblolly Bay *398*
Monodelphia Polyandria
Bulstrode 6.10.77

99 *Gorteria Rigens* Narrow leav'd Gorteria *399*
Syngenesia Polyg. Frustania
St James's Place 27.5.79
Prov: Dr Pitcairn

100 *Gorteria Ciliaris 400*
Syng. Polyg. Frust.
St James's Place 5.78
Prov: Kew

Volume V

1 *Grewia Occidentalis 401*
Gynandria Polyandria
Bulstrode 29.10.77
Prov: Kew

2 *Gypsophila Prostrata 402*
St James's Place 31.8.78
Prov: Dr Pitcairn

3 *Hebenstretia Dentata 403*
Didynamia Giospermia
Bulstrode 12.12.76
Prov: Kew

4 *Hedysarum Onobrychis* St Foin, French
   Honeysuckle *404*
Bulstrode 23.6.80

5 *Hedysarum Alp 405*
St James's Place 2.5.78
Prov: Kew

6 *Hedysarum Canescens* Hoary French Honeysuckle
   406
Bulstrode 9.9.80

7 *Hedysarum Vespertillio* Bat-leav'd French
   honeysuckle *407*
St James's Place 7.10.80

8 *Hedysarum Movens* Moving Plant *408*
Diadelphia Decandria
Luton Park 22.6.78

9 *Helleborus Faetidus* Black hellebore, Great
   Bearsfoot *409*
Polyandria Polygynia
St James's Place 25.3.78
Prov: Bulstrode

10 *Helleborus Virides* Green hellebore *410*
St James's Place 20.3.78

11 *Helleborus Hyemalis* Winter aconite *411*
Polyandria polygynia
St James's Place 19.2.77
Prov: Wimbledon

12 *Helleborus Niger* Christmas Rose *412*
Polyandria Polygynia
St James's Place

13 *Helianthus Annuus* Great Sun-flower *413*

14 *Helenium Autumnale* Autumnal Bastard
   Sunflower *414*
Bulstrode 7.9.81

15 *Heliotropium Peruvianum* Turnsole *415*
Pentandria Monogynia
St James's Place 7.5.78
Prov: Ld Dartmouth, Black Heath

16 *Helonias Asphodeloides 416*
Hexandria Trigynia
Bulstrode 3.7.77

17 *Haemanthus Puniceus* Bloodflower *417*
Bulstrode 28.6.80

18 *Hemanthus Coccineus* Scarlet Blood-flower *418*
Hexandria Monogynia
Luton 19.8.76

18 *Hemanthus Coccineus* Leaves and root belonging
   to the Blood Flower *418**

19 *Hemerocallis Fulva* Bruno's Lilly *419*
Bulstrode 25.7.80

20 *Hemerocallis Flava* Day Lily *420*
Bulstrode 14.6.79

21 *Hermannia Lavendulaefolia 421*
Monodelphia Pentandria
Bulstrode 12.11.78
Prov: Kew

22 *Hermania Althaeifolia 422*
Monodelphia Pentandria
Bulstrode 19.9.77

23 *Hesperis Tristis* Melancholly Stock *423*
Tetradynia Siliquosa
Bulstrode 4.9.77
Prov: Luton

24 *Hibiscus Syriacus 424*
Monodelphia Polyandria
Bulstrode 22.9.77

25 *Hibiscus Manihot 425*
Monadelphia Polyandria
Luton 14.8.77

26 *Hibiscus Malvaviscus 426*
Monadelphia Polyandria
Bulstrode 22.11.75

27 *Hibiscus Rosa Sinensis* China Rose *427*
Monadelphia Polyandria
Luton 21.8.77

28 *Hibiscus Rosa Sinensis* Double China Rose *428*
Monodelphia Polyandr:
7.75
Prov: Bulstrode

29 *Hieracium Dubium* Creeping Smooth
   Hawkweed *429*
Bulstrode 11.9.79

30 *Hieracium Auranhacum* Grim the Collier *430*
Syngenesia Polyg: Aequa:
Bulstrode 30.9.79

31 *Holosteum Umbellatum* Smooth umbel
   Chickweed *431*
Bulstrode 19.6.80

32 *Hottonia Palustris* Water Violet *432*
Pentandria Monogynia
Bulstrode 18.5.75

33 *Humulus Lupulus* The Hop *433*
Bulstrode 18.8.81

34 *Hyacinthus Orientalis* Double Pink Hyacinth *434*
St James's Place 22.3.76

35 *Hyacinthus Orientalis* Prince William *435*
St James's Place 25.4.80
Prov: The Revd. Mr Lawrence

36 *Hyacinthus Orientalis Ophir* Yellow ophir
   hyacinth *436*
St James's Place 5.5.80
Prov: Lord Harcourt

37 *Hyacinthus Orientalis* Mount Vesuvias *437*
St James's Place 5.3.77
Prov: Mr Lawrence's, Mount Vesuvias

38 *Hyacinthus Viridis* Green hyacinth *438*
St James's Place 11.10.80
Prov: Kew

39 *Hydrocharis Morsus Rana* Frog bit *439*
Bulstrode 8.78

40 *Hyoscyamus Aureus* Henbane of Crete *440*
Pentandria Monogynia
St James's Place 2.6.77
Prov: Barnes

41 *Hyoseris Radiata 441*

42 *Hypericum Humifusum* Trailing St John's-wort
   442
Bulstrode 9.8.80

43 *Hypericum Pulchrum* Elegant St John's-wort *443*
Bulstrode 15.7.80

44 *Hypericum Perfoliatum 444*
Bulstrode 15.8.80

45 *Hypericum Prolificum* St John's wort *445*
Polyadelphia Polyandria
Bulstrode 12.9.77
Prov: Kew

46 *Hypericum Monogynum* Chinese St John's wort
   446
Polyadelphia Polyandria
Bulstrode 4.8.76

47 *Hypericum Androsaemum* Tutsan or park Leaves
   447
Bulstrode 23.7.79

48 *Hypericum Ascyron* Great flower'd St John's wort
   448
Bulstrode 12.8.80

49 *Hypoxis Erecta* Bastard Star of Bethlehem *449*
St James's Place 17.8.79
Prov: Mr Lee

50 *Jasminum Grandiflorum* Catalonian Jasmine *450*
Diandria Monogynia
Bulstrode 3.9.[?]
Prov: Sion [House], D of Northumberland

51 *Jasminum Lanceolatum* Simple-leav'd Jasmine,
   Solandri *451*
St James's Place 14.8.79
Prov: Mr Lee

52 *Jasminum Odoratissimum* Yellow Indian Jasmine
   452
Diandria Monogynia
Bulstrode 25.10.77

53 *Jasminum Officinale* White Jasmine *453*

54 *Jasminum Azorium* Azorian jasmine *454*
Diandria Monogynia
Bill Hill 27.8.76

55 *Iatropha Multifida* Scarlet flower'd Physic-nut
   455
Bulstrode 6.9.81

56 *Iberis Semperflorens* Tree Candy-tuft *456*
Tetradynamia Siliculosa
Bulstrode 20.11.78
Prov: Kew

57 *Iberis Amara* White bitter Candy-tuft *457*
   Tetradynamia Siliculosa
Bulstrode 1.11.76

58 *Illecebrum Verticillatum* Knot grass *458*
Pentandria Monogynia
Bulstrode 17.9.76

59 *Ilex Angustifolia* Narrow leaved Holly *459*
Bulstrode 1.11.79

60 *Ilex Aquifolium* Holly *460*
Tetandria tetragynia
Bulstrode 24.11.75

61 *Illicium Anisatum* Starry anniseed *461*
Dodecandria Octogyn
St James's Place 20.3.76

62 *Impatiens Noli Mi Tangere* Impatient Balsam *462*
Bulstrode 5.8.[?]

63 *Impatiens Noli Tangere* Touch me not,
   Americana *463*
Syngenesia Monogynia

64 *Indigo Fera* from ye Cape, Non descript Indigo
464
Diadelphia Decandria
St James's Place 18.4.77
Prov: Kew

65 *Indigo Fera Coriacea Solandri 465*
Diadelphia Decor;
Bulstrode 21.11.78
Prov: Kew

66 *Inula Helenium, Elecampane 466*
Bulstrode 25.7.78

67 *Inula Dysenterica*, Fleabane *467*
Bulstrode 8.9.81

68 *Ipomea Coccinea*, Scarlet flower'd Ipomea *468*

69 *Ipomea Quamoclit 469*
Pentandria Monogynia
Bulstrode 7.78

70 *Iris Pseudacorus* Yellow iris *470*
Triandria Monogynia
Bulstrode 1.7.77

71 *Iris Xiphium* Bulbous rooted Iris *471*
Bulstrode 27.6.80

72 *Iris Ochroleuca 472*
Triandria Monogynia
Bulstrode 2.7.77

73 *Iris Squalens* Dingy flower de Luce *473*
Triandria Monogynia
Bulstrode 26.6.76

74 *Iris Christata Solander 474*
St James's Place 28.5.78
Prov: Dr Pitcairn

75 *Iris Persica* Persian Iris *475*
Triandria Monogyn.
St James's Place 19.3.76

76 *Iris Sambucina* Elder scented *476*
Bulstrode 22.6.80
Prov: Weymouth

77 *Iris Susiana* Chalcedonian *477*
St James's Place 12.5.81
Prov: Mrs Pultney

78 *Justicia Ecbolium 478*
Diandria Monogynia
Bulstrode 5.8.77
Prov: Luton

79 *Justicia Hyssopifolia 479*
Diandria Monogynia
Bulstrode 30.6.78
Prov: Luton

80 *Ixia Longiflora 480*
Triandria Monogynia
St James's Place 20.5.79
Prov: Dr Pitcairn

81 *Ixia Bulbifera 481*
Triandria Monogynia
St James's Place 29.4.79
Prov: Mr Lee

82 *Ixia Sceptrum Solandri* Sceptre Ixia *482*
St James's Place 26.4.79
Prov: Mr B. Grey

83 *Ixia Chinensis 483*
Bulstrode 26.8.80

84 *Ixia Crocata 484*
Triandria Monogynia
St James's Place 15.5.78
Prov: Kew

85 *Kalmia Latifolia 485*
Decandria Monogynia
Bulstrode 6.75

86 *Kalmia Angustifolia* Narrow leav'd Kalmia *486*
Decandria Monogynia
Bulstrode 24.6.76

87 *Kalmia Glauca 487*
St James's Place 22.4.79
Prov: Chelsea Physic Garden

88 *Kaempferia Galanga* Round leav'd *488*
Monandria Monogynia
Bulstrode 23.7.76

89 *Lagerstroemia Indica* Indian Lagerstroemia *489*
St James's Place 27.7.81
Prov: Kew

90 *Lamium Album* Arch Angel *490*
Bulstrode 8.11.79

91 *Lantana* Non descript *491*
Didynamia Angiosp:

92 *Lantana Trifolia 492*
Didynam: Angios:
Bulstrode 28.10.77

93 *Lantana Involucrata 493*
Bulstrode 18.10.79
Prov: Mr Lee

94 *Lantana Aculeata 494*
Didynam. Angios.
Bulstrode 13.11.77

95 *Lantana Africana* Ilex leav'd Jesamine *495*
Pentandria Monogynia
Bulstrode 17.11.77

96 *Lathraea Squamaria* Toothwort *496*
St James's Place 28.4.81
Prov: Bulstrode

97 *Lathyrus Sativus* Blue Gard: Chicky vetch *497*
Diadelphia Decandria
Bill Hill 23.8.76
Prov: Luton Park

98 *Lathyrus Sylvestris* Narrow Pease Everlasting *498*
Bulstrode 8.8.80

99 *Lathyrus Odoratus* Sweet pea *499*
Decadelphia decandria
Bulstrode 9.10.77

100 *Lathyrus Aphacea*, Yellow vetchling *500*
Bulstrode 6.10.78

Volume VI

1 *Lathyrus Latifolius* Broad-leav'd Everlasting Pea
501
Bulstrode 22.8.81

2 *Lathyrus Palustris* Marsh Chickling Vetch *502*
Bulstrode 19.6.79

3 *Lavandula Multifida 503*
Didynamia Gynosp;
St James's Place 8.8.77

4 *Lavatera Trimestris 504*
Monodelphia Polyandria
Bulstrode 1774

5 *Lavatera Olbia 505*
Monodelphia Polyandria
Bulstrode 4.7.78

6 *Ledum Latifolium* Swedish Tea *506*
St James's Place 28.4.79
Prov: Chelsea Physic Garden

7 *Ledum Thymifolium Solandri 507*
Decandria Monogynia
Bulstrode 1779

8 *Leontodon Autumnale* Yellow Devil's Bit *508*
Bulstrode 16.8.80

9 *Leonorus Tataricus 509*
Didynamia Gymnospermia
Bulstrode 20.9.77
Prov: Kew

10 *Lepidium Alpinum* Greater Snow drop *510*
Tetradinamia Siliculosa
Bulstrode 14.10.77
Prov: Kew

11 *Leucojum Astivum* Summer Snow-drop *511*
St James's Place 9.5.78
Prov: Islington

12 *Lightfootia Canescens* New genus Solander *512*
Tetradynamia Siliculos
Bulstrode 29.10.78
Prov: Kew

13 *Ligustrum Vulgare* Privet *513*
Bulstrode 11.7.80

14 *Lilium Canadense 514*
St James's Place 20.8.79
Prov: Mr Lee

15 *Lilium Byzantinum* Byzantin Lily *515*
St James's Place 8.6.81
Prov: Mr Lee

16 *Limodorum Tuberosum 516*
Gynandria Diandria
Bulstrode 13.10.75

17 *Linnea Borealis 517*
Didym: Angeosp:
Bulstrode 24.11.78

18 *Linum Angustifolium* Narrow leav'd Flax *518*
Bulstrode 7.8.80

19 *Linum Angustifolium*, Narrow leav'd Flax *519*

20 *Linum Maritimum*, Sea Flax *520*
St James's Place 3.10.80
Prov: Dr Pitcairn, Islington

21 *Liriodendron Tulipifera*, Tulip Tree *521*
Polyandria Polygynia
Bulstrode 5.7.76

22 *Lisianthus Sempervirens 522*
St James's Place 22.12.79
Prov: Lord Bute

23 *Lithospermum Purpurocaruleum*, purple Gromwil
523
Pentandria Monogynia
Bulstrode 6.6.77

24 *Lobelia Acaulis Solandri 524*
Syngenesia Monogamia
Bulstrode 26.6.77

25 *Lobelia Erinoides 525*
Singenesia Monogamia
Bulstrode 3.9.[?]
Prov: Luton, Ld Bute

26 *Lobelia Urens 526*
Syngenesia Monogamia
Bulstrode 10.75

27 *Lobelia Coronopifolia* Cape of Good Hope,
   Solander *527*
St James's Place 4.79
Prov: Kew

28 *Lobelia Siphiletica* Blue Virgin Lobelia *528*
Syngenesia Monogamia
Bulstrode 8.9.76

29 *Lobelia Cardinalis* Scarlet Cardinal Flower *529*
St James's Place 4.10.80
Prov: Dr Pitcairn

29 *Scarlet Geranium Lobelia Cardinalis 529**
Bulstrode 1773

30 *Lobelia Pubescens* Downy Cardinal-flower *530*
St James's Place 17.5.81
Prov: Kew

31 *Lonicera Caprifolium* Scarlet trumpet honey
   suckle *531*
Pentandria Monogynia
Bulstrode 3.9.76

32 *Lonicera periclymenum* Woodbine or Honeysuckle
   532
Pentandria Monogynia
St James's Place

33 *Lonicera Pyrenaica* Red Fly Honeysuckle *533*
Pentandria Monogynia
St James's Place 14.5.76

34 *Lonicera Carulea* Blue-berried Fly Honeysuckle
   534
Bulstrode 21.10.80

35 *Lotus Jacobaeus 535*
Bulstrode 20.10.79
Prov: Mr Lee

36 *Lotus Hirsutus 536*
Bulstrode 20.10.80

37 *Lotus Dorycnium* Small white flower'd lotus *537*
Diadelphia decandria
Bulstrode 23.11.76

38 *Lotus Arabicus 538*
Diadelphia Decandria
Luton 28.8.77

39 *Lotus Tetragonolobus* Scarlet winged pea *539*
Diadelphia Decandria
Bulstrode 26.10.75

40 *Ludwigia Ovata* Oval leav'd Ludwigia *540*
Bulstrode 10.8.80

41 *Lupinus Luteus* Yellow Lupine *541*
St James's Place

42 *Lupinus Varius* Blue Lupine *542*
Bulstrode 1774

43 *Lupinus Hirsutus* Hairy Lupin *543*
Diadelphia Decandria
Bulstrode 4.10.76

44 *Lychnis Dioica* White Campion *544*
Bulstrode 26.6.79

45 *Lychnis Chalcedonica* Scarlet lychnis *545*
Decandria Pentagynia
Bulstrode 7.75

46 *Lychnis* Red flower'd species, non-descript *546*
Decandria Pentagynia
St James's Place 19.4.77
Prov: Kew

47 *Lycium Afrum*, African Box-thorn *547*
St James's Place 22.4.80
Prov: Bulstrode

48 *Lysimachia Virgata Solander* Loosestrife *548*
Pentandria Monogynia
Bulstrode 7.78
Prov: Luton

49 *Lysimachia Vulgaris* Yellow loosestrife *549*
Bulstrode 30.7.78

50 *Lysimachia Valicifolia* Willow leav'd Loosestrife
   550
Bulstrode 13.9.80

51 *Lysimachia* Thirsiflora Globe loosestrife *551*
Bulstrode 13.6.80

52 *Lysimachia Nummularia* Herb Twopence *552*
Pentandria Monogynia
Bulstrode 14.7.77

53 *Lythrum Salicaria* Willow herb *553*
Bulstrode 1.8.79

54 *Magnolia Glauca* Swamp magnolia *554*
Polyandria Polygynia
Bulstrode 18.7.7[?]

55 *Magnolia Acuminata* B lue Magnolia *555*
St James's Place 13.5.79
Prov: Kew

56 *Magnolia Tripetala* Umbrella Tree *556*
Polyandria Polygynia
St James's Place 12.5.79
Prov: Kew

57 *Magnolia Grandiflora* The grand Magnolia *557*
Polyandria Polygynia
Bill Hill 26.8.76

58 *Mahernia Pinnata 558*
Pentandria Pentagynia
Bulstrode 10.10.77
Prov: Kew

59 *Malpighia Urens 559*
Decandria Trigynia
Bulstrode 15.10.77

60 *Malpighia Canescens* Yellow flower'd hoary
   leav'd *560*
Bulstrode 10.76

61 *Malpighia Glabra* Smooth leav'd *561*
Decandria Trygynia
Bulstrode 16.9.76

62 *Malva Sylvestris* Common Mallow *562*
Bulstrode 6.8.81

63 *Malva Sylvestris* Common Malow *563*
Monodelphia Polyandria
Bulstrode 11.76

64 *Malva Verticillata* Whirl'd Mallow *564*
Bulstrode 6.7.80

65 *Malva Maschata* Jagged Musk Mallow *565*
Monodelphia Polyandria
Bulstrode 23.9.76

66 *Manuelea Tomentosa 566*
Didynamia Angiospermia
Bulstrode 10.77
Prov: Kew

67 *Martynia Perennis 567*
Bulstrode 19.10.75

68 *Matricaria Parthenium* Fever few *568*
Bulstrode 6.8.78

69 *Medicago Sativa* Lucern *569*
Bulstrode 5.8.80

70 *Melampyrum Christatum* Cow wheat *570*
Bulstrode 13.7.78

71 *Melia Azedarach* Bead tree *571*
Decandria Monogynia
St James's Place 5.5.78
Prov: Lord Dartmouth, Blackheath

72 *Melissa Nepeta* Calamint *572*
Bulstrode 5.75

73 *Melittis Melissophyllum* Bastard Balm *573*
Didynamia Gymnospermia
Bulstrode 5.75

74 *Menyanthes Nymphoides* Fringed water lily *574*
Pentandria Monogynia
Bulstrode 15.9.77

75 *Meneanthis Trifoliata* Water trefoil *575*
Pentandria Monogynia
Bulstrode 5.75

76 *Mesembryanthemum Tenuifolium* Scarlet fricoides
   576
Icosandria Pentagynia
Bulstrode 17.6.76

77 *Mesembryanthemum Planum Solandri* New species
   577
Icosandria Pentagynia
St James's Place 28.3.78
Prov: Islington, Dr Pitcairn

78 *Mesembrianthemum Aureum Solandri* New species
   578
St James's Place 17.5.80
Prov: Chelsea Physic Garden

79 *Mesembryanthemum Splendens 579*
Icosandria Pentagynia
Bulstrode 4.8.78

80 *Mesembryanthemum Hispidum 580*
Icosandria Pentagynia
Bulstrode 22.7.77

81 *Messpilus Germanica* Medlar *581*
Icosandria Pentagynia
Bulstrode 24.9.77

82 *Mespilus Amelanchier* Snowy *582*
St James's Place 5.77

83 *Mespilus Piracantha* Fiery-thorn *583*
Bulstrode 17.6.80

84 *Mimosa Latsiliqua* White flowering accasia with
   broad pods *584*
Polygamia Monoecia
Bulstrode 12.9.76

85 *Mimosa Farnesiana 585*
Polygamia Monoecia
Bulstrode 10.77

86 *Mimosa Arborea 586*
Bulstrode 28.9.79
Prov: Mr Bateman's, Old Windsor

87 *Mirabilis Longiflora* Marvel of Peru *587*
Pentandria Monogynia
Bill Hill 28.8.76

88 *Mitella Diphylla* Bastard An: Sanicle *588*
St James's Place 8.5.78
Prov: Dr Pitcairn, Islington

89 *Moluccella Laevis* Molucca Balm *589*
Didynamia Gynospermia
Luton 7.77
Prov: Lord Bute

90 *Monarda Fistulosa 590*
Diandria Monogynia
Bulstrode 7.77

91 *Monarda Oblongata* Dr Solander *591*
Bulstrode 4.9.81

92 *Myosotis Scorpiodes* Mouse-ear Scorpion Grass *592*
Polyandria Monogynia
Wellesbourne 12.7.75

93 *Myrtus Communis* The Myrtle-tree *593*
Bulstrode 23.8.81

94 *Narcissus Jonquilla Plena* Double jonquill *594*
St James's Place 17.5.80

95 *Narcissus Poeticus* The Poet's Narcissus *595*
Hexandria Monogynia
St James's Place 7.3.78

96 *Narcissus Tazetta* A variety *596*
Hexandria Monogynia
St James's Place 20.1.76

97 *Narcissus* Var. White *597*
St James's Place 7.3.76

98 *Narcissus Tazetta* Polyanthus Narcissus *598*
Hexan. Monogynia
St James's Place 22.1.76

99 *Narcissus Papyraceus* A Variety Starry *599*
St James's Place 11.3.76

100 *Nerium Oleander* Common Rosebay *600*
Bulstrode 24.8.80

Volume VII

1 *Nicotiana Tabacum* Tobacco *601*
Bulstrode 25.9.80

2 *Nigella Hispanica* Fennel flowd, or devil in a Bush *602*
Bulstrode 2.10.78

3 *Nigella Damascena* Devil in a Bush *603*

4 *Nolana Prostrata 604*
Pentandria Monogynia
Bulstrode 10.6.77

5 *Nictanthes Sambac* Double Arabian Jasmine *605*
Bulstrode 30.8.80

6 *Nyctanthes Sambac* Arabian Jasmine *606*
Bulstrode 30.8.80

7 *Nymphaea Alba* White water lilly *607*
Polyandria Monogynia
Bulstrode 31.7.76

8 *Nymphaea Lutea* Yellow water lilly *608*
Polyandria Monogynia
Bulstrode 2.8.76

9 *Ocymum Rugosurp 609*
Didynamia Gymnosperm.
Bulstrode 10.10.77
Prov: Kew

10 *Oenothera Grandiflora* Night primrose *610*
Bulstrode 14.10.80
Prov: Chelsea Physic Garden

11 *Oenothera Longiflora* Tree primrose *611*
Bulstrode 22.9.78

12 *Oenothera Pumila* Dwarf evening primrose *612*
Octandria Monogynia
Bulstrode

13 *Oenanthe Pimpinelloides 613*
Bulstrode 9.79

14 *Olea Capensis* The Cape Olive *614*
Bulstrode 1780

15 *Olea Odoratissima* Solander Qui fa from China *615*
Diandria Monogynia
St James's Place 26.5.77
Prov: Dr Pitcairn, Islington

16 *Onopordum Acanthium* Cotton thistle *616*
Bulstrode 21.8.80

17 *Ononis Fruticosa* Rest Harrow *617*
Bulstrode 1.7.78

18 *Ophioxylon Serpentinum 618*
Tetrandria Monogynia
Bulstrode 9.8.76

19 *Ophrys Anthropophora* Green man orchis *619*
Gynandria Dynandria
Bulstrode 12.7.77

20 *Ophris Apifera* Bee orchis *620*
Bulstrode 11.6.79

21 *Ophrys Insectifera* var Myodes Fly Ophrys *621*
Bulstrode 13.6.80

22 *Ophris Spiralis* Ladies tresses *622*
Gynandria Dyandria
Bulstrode 14.9.76

23 *Orchis Bifolia* Butterfly Orchis *623*
Bulstrode 5.6.79

24 *Ophris Nidus Avis* Bird's Nest Ophrys *624*
St James's Place 6.79

25 *Orchis Pyramidalis* Purple late orchis *625*
Bulstrode 7.7.80

26 *Orchis Mascula* Spotted handed Orchis *626*
Gynandria Diandria
St James's Place 27.4.79
Prov: Bulstrode

27 *Orchis Maculata* Male spotted Orchis *627*
Ginandria Diandria
Bulstrode 6.77

28 *Orchis Ustulata* Dwarf orchis *628*
Gynandria Diandria
Bulstrode 3.6.79

29 *Orchis Militaris* True Man Orchis *629*
Bulstrode 15.6.80

30 *Lizard Orchis* Italian Man Orchis *630*

31 *Ornithogalum Nutans 631*
St James's Place 27.4.78

32 *Ornithogalum Narbonense* Star of Bethm: *632*
St James's Place 6.78
Prov: Bulstrode, Mr Yalden

33 *Ornithogalum Luteum* Star of Bethlem: *633*
Hexandria Monogynia
St James's Place 6.4.78

34 *Ornithogalum Pyramidale* Star of Bethlem *634*
Bulstrode 6.79

35 *Ornithogalum Pyrenaicum* Greenish Star of Bethlehem *635*
Bulstrode 17.6.79

36 *Ornithogalum Arabicum* Arabian Star of Bethlehem *636*
Hexandria Monogynia
St James's Place 3.2.79
Prov: Bulstrode

37 *Orobus Sylvaticus* Bitter Wood Vetch *637*
Diadelphia Decandria
Bulstrode 4.6.77

38 *Osteospermum Spinosum 638*
Syngen: Polygam: Necessari
Bulstrode 11.77

39 *Oxalis Acetosella* White wood sorrel *639*
Decandria Pentagynia
Bulstrode 5.75

40 *Oxalis Acetosella* Wood Sorrel var Purple *640*
Decandria Pentagynia
Bulstrode 5.75

41 *Oxalis Corniculata* Yellow wood sorrel *641*
Bulstrode 18.9.79

42 *Oxalis Pes Capri 642*
St James's Place 14.4.79
Prov: Upton, Essex, Dr Fothergill

43 *Oxalis Affrica* Solandri Wood sorrel *643*
Decandria Pentagynia
St James's Place 26.3.78
Prov: Islington, Dr Pitcairn

44 *Paeonia Tenuifolia* Fine leav'd Piony *644*
St James's Place 5.78
Prov: Kew

45 *Pancratium Maritimum* Sea Daffodil *645*
Hexandria Monogynia
St James's Place 2.78
Prov: Bulstrode

46 *Papaver Cambricum* Yellow Welch Poppy *646*
Polyandria Monogynia
Bulstrode 1774

47 *Papaver Rheus* Common Corn Poppy *647*
Bulstrode 10.79

48 *Papaver Somniferum* The Opium Poppy *648*
Polyandria Monogynia
Bulstrode 18.10.76

49 *Paris Quadrifolia* True Love *649*
St James's Place 13.5.78

50 *Parnassia Palustris* Grass of Parnassus *650*
Pentandria Tetragynia
Bulstrode 13.9.76

51 *Passiflora Rubra 651*
Gynandria Pentandria
Bulstrode 17.10.77

52 *Passiflora Holosericea 652*
Gynandria Pentagynia
Bulstrode 27.9.77

53 *Passiflora Murucuja 653*
Gymnos: Pentagynia
Bulstrode 23.9.77

54 *Passiflora Laurifolia* Bay Leaved *654*
Gynandria Pentandria
Luton 8.77
Prov: Lord Bute

55 *Passiflora Cerulea* Common Passion Flower *655*
Bulstrode 6.79

56 *Passiflora Quadrangularis* Granadillos *656*
St James's Place 12.6.78

57 *Passerina Filiformis* Ethiopian Sparrow-wort *657*
Octandria Monogynia
St James's Place 2.5.81
Prov: Bulstrode

58 *Petiveria Alliacea 658*
Bulstrode 7.11.78

59 *Phaseolus Coccineus* Scarlet kidney-bean *659*
Diadelphia Decandria
Bill Hill 29.8.76

60 *Phaseolus Caracalla 660*
Bulstrode 21.10.79
Prov: Mr Lee

61 *Philadelphus Aromaticus Solander* New Zealand
Tea *661*
St James's Place 6.78
Prov: Chelsea Physic Garden

62 *Phlomis Leonorus* Lion's Tail *662*
Didynam: Gymnos:
Bulstrode 10.77

63 *Phlomis Zeilanica 663*
Didynamia Gymnos:
Bulstrode 31.10.77
Prov: Kew

64 *Phlox Carolina 664*
Pentandria Monogynia
Bulstrode 1774

65 *Phlox Divaricata 665*
St James's Place 24.4.79
Prov: Chelsea Physic Garden

66 *Phlox Undulata* Great Lychnidea *666*
Bulstrode 11.8.81

67 *Phlox Suaveolens 667*
Decandria Pentagyn
Bulstrode 10.6.76

68 *Phyllanthus Epiphyllanthus 668*
Monecia Triandria
Bulstrode 3.7.78
Prov: Luton, Lord Bute

69 *Physalis Pubescens 669*
Pentandria Monogynia
Bulstrode 10.79
Prov: Kew

70 *Physalis Cretica Solandri 670*
Pentandria Monogynia
Bulstrode 13.10.77
Prov: Kew, Dower: Lady Gower

71 *Physalis Alkekengi* Winter cherry [Flower] *671*
Pentandria Monogynia

71a *Physalis* Winter cherry [Berry] *672*
Bulstrode November

72 *Physalis Somnifera* Sleepy Bladder Nightshade
673
Bulstrode 7.11.76

73 *Phylica Ericoides* Bastard Aleternus *674*
Pentandria Monogynia
St James's Place 31.1.78
Prov: Black Heath

74 *Phyteuma Orbicularis* Horned Rampions *675*

75 *Phytolacca Icosandra* American nightshade *676*
Bulstrode 3.10.78

76 *Pimpinella Saxifraga* Burnet leav'd *677*
Bulstrode 15.11.79

77 *Pinguicula Vulgaris* Common Butterwort *678*
Bulstrode 20.6.80

78 *Piper Stellatum Solandri* A new species *679*
Bulstrode 16.10.79
Prov: Mr Lee

79 *Pisum Marinum* Sea Pea *680*
Bulstrode 13.9.79
Prov: Weymouth

80 *Pisum Sativum* Garden Pease *681*
Bulstrode 14.11.76

81 *Plumeria Rubra* Red Plumeria *682*
Pentandria Monogynia
Bulstrode 7.8.76
Prov: Bulstrode

82 *Plumbago Zeylanica* Ceylon lead-wort *683*
Bulstrode 21.9.80

83 *Poinciana Pulcherrima* Barbados flowerfence *684*
Decandria Monogynia
Bulstrode 10.78
Prov: Sion [House], D of Northumberland

84 *Ipomea Rubra 685*
Prov: Bulstrode

85 *Polyanthus Tuberosa* Tuberose *686*
Hexandria Monogynia
Bulstrode 1.10.76

86 *Polygala Myrtifolia* African milkwort *687*
Diadelphia Octandria
Luton 21.8.77
Prov: Lord Bute

87 *Polygala Chamabuxus* Box-leav'd Milk-wort *688*
Bulstrode 8.9.81

88 *Polygonum Orientale* Oriental Persicaria *689*
Bill Hill 30.8.79

89 *Polygonum Viviparum* Viviparous Bistort *690*
Bulstrode 10.6.79

90 *Polyganum Fagopyrum* Buckwheat *691*
Bulstrode 8.80

91 *Portlandia Grandiflora 692*
Bulstrode 9.8.82
Prov: Kew

92 *Potentilla Rupestris* Rock Cinquefoil *693*
Bulstrode 2.7.79

93 *Potentilla Recta* Upright cinquefoil *694*
Icosandria Polygynia
Bulstrode 18.10.77

94 *Potentilla Fruticosa* Shrubby cinquefoil *695*
Bulstrode

95 *Potentilla Alba* White cinquefoil *696*
Bulstrode 3.11.77

96 *Poterium Spinosum* Prickly Burnet *697*
St James's Place 5.4.79

97 *Primula Auricula* Bear's Ear *698*
Pentandria Monogynia
St James's Place 18.4.77
Prov: Kew

98 *Primula Auricula* var: *699*
St James's Place 22.3.79

99 *Primula Auricula* var: *700*
St James's Place 3.4.78
Prov: Mrs Dashwood

100 *Primula Auricula* var: Double yellow auricula
701
St James's Place 29.4.78
Prov: Mrs Dashwood

Volume VIII

1 *Primula Polyanthus Elatior* var Primrose *702*
Hexandria Monogynia
St James's Place 4.75

2 *Primula Vulgaris Acaulis 703*
Pentandria Monogynia
St James's Place 4.75

3 *Primula Veris* Cowslip *704*
Pentandria Monogynia
St James's Place 4.75

4 *Primula Veris Elatior* Oxslip *705*
Pentandria Monogynia
St James's Place 29.4.77

5 *Primula* var. Double Primroses *706*
St James's Place 11.4.78

6 *Prunus Domestica* Plumb *707*
St James's Place 24.3.79

7 *Prunus Spinosa* Blackthorn *708*
St James's Place 25.3.79

8 *Prunus Cerasus* Double flowering cherry a var.
709
Icosan: Monog
St James's Place 3.5.76

9 *Prunus Arminiaca* Apricot *710*
St James's Place 23.3.79

10 *Prunella Grandiflora* Great Selfheal *711*
Bulstrode 29.8.81

11 *Psoralea Palestina 712*
Bulstrode 28.8.80

12 *Psoralia Angustifolia Solandri* New species *713*
Diadelphia Decandria
Bulstrode 19.11.77
Prov: Kew

13 *Psoralia Ethiopia Pinnata 714*
Diadelphia Decandria
Bulstrode 8.77
Prov: Lord Bute, Luton

14 *Pulmonaria Paniculata Solandri 715*
Bulstrode 22.9.79
Prov: Kew

15 *Punica Nana* Dwarf Pomegranate *716*
Icosandria Monogynia
Bulstrode 13.8.78

16 *Punica Granatum* Pomegranate *717*
St James's Place 12.9.78
Prov: Chelsea Physic Garden

17 *Pyrus Communis* Common Pear *718*
St James's Place 14.5.78
Prov: Ealing

18 *Pyrus Malus* Apple Blo: *719*
St James's Place 5.5.78
Prov: Whitehall, Dwr Dss of Portland,

19 *Pyrus Cydonia* Quince *720*
St James's Place 13.5.76

20 *Quercus Robur* The Oak-tree with short stalk'd
    Acorns *721*
Bulstrode 9.81

21 *Ranunculus Aquaticus* Water crowfoot *722*
Polyandria Polygynia
St James's Place 26.4.76

22 *Ranunculus Ficaria* Lesser pilewort *723*
St James's Place 15.3.79
Ealing

23 *Ranunculus Lingua* Great spearwort *724*
Bulstrode 31.7.79

24 *Ranunculus Flammula* Procumbent spearwort
    725
St James's Place 12.8.79

25 *Ranunculus Illyricus* *726*
Polyandria Polygynia
St James's Place 1.5.79
Prov: Chelsea Physic Garden

26 *Ranunculus Asiaticus* var Garden ranunculus *727*
St James's Place 21.5.76

27 *Reseda Odorata* Minionette *728*
St James's Place 10.2.78

28 *Rhexia Virginica* *729*
Octandria Monogynia
Bulstrode 17.9.77
Prov: Kew

29 *Rhodora Canadensis* *730*
Bulstrode 7.79

30 *Rhodendron Maximum* Dwarf rose bay *731*
Luton 25.6.78

31 *Rhododendron Ponticum* Purple flowered rose bay
    732
Luton Park 9.6.78

32 *Rhododendron Ferrugineum* *733*
Decandria Monogynia
St James's Place 29.5.77
Prov: Mr B. Grey

33 *Rivina Laevis* *734*
Bulstrode 7.79

34 *Robinia Pseudacacia* White bastard acacia *735*
Dyadelphia Decandria
Bulstrode 3.6.76

35 *Robinia Hispida* Red hairy robinia *736*
Diadelphia Decandria
Bulstrode 22.6.[?]

36 *Rosa Eglanteria?* Yellow rose *737*
Icosindria Polygynia
Bulstrode 1.7.74

37 *Rosa Alpina* Halifax *738*
Bill Hill 26.8.79

38 *Rosa Gallica* Cluster damask rose *739*
Bulstrode 7.80

39 *Rosa Gallica* Moss Provence *740*
Icosandria Polygynia
Bulstrode 6.75

40 *Rosa Gallica* Blush rose *741*
Icosandria Polygynia
Bulstrode 7.74

41 *Rosa Gallica* White rose *742*
St James's Place 27.6.81
Prov: Lady Weymouth

42 *Rosa Semper Virens* Ever green musk rose *743*
Icosandria Polygynia
Bulstrode 21.9.76

43 *Rosa Sempervirens* Rose de Meaux *744*

44 *Rosa Spinosissima* Cyphian rose *745*
Bulstrode 20.6.77

45 *Rosa Spinosissima* Burnet rose *746*
Icosandria Polygynia
Bulstrode 11.11.76

46 *Rosa Canina* Dog rose *747*
Bulstrode 24.6.77

47 *Rosa Villosa* Apple rose *748*
Icosandria Polygynia
Bulstrode 6.75

48 *Rosa Fluvialis ?* Flora Danica Lady Stamford's
    rose *749*
Bulstrode 1775

49 *Rubus Saxatilis* Stone bramble *750*
Bulstrode 4.6.79

50 *Rubus Caesius* Dewberry *751*
Icosandria Polygynia
Bulstrode 21.10.77

51 *Rubus Fruiticosus* Common bramble *752*
Icosandria Polygynia
Welsbourn 13.7.75

52 *Rubus Odoratus* Sweet flowering rasberry
    [American] *753*

53 *Rudbeckia Trifoliata* *754*
Bulstrode 8.10.79

54 *Rudbeckia Purpurea* With pendant petals *755*
Syngenisia Polygamia Frustianea
Bulstrode 10.8.76

55 *Ruseus Aculeatus* Butcher's broom *756*
Dioecia Singenesia
Bulstrode 25.11.77

56 *Ruta Chalopensis* Rue *757*
Decandria Monogynia
St James's Place 24.4.77
Prov: Kew

57 *Sagina Erecta* Little upright stitchwort *758*
Tetrandia Tetragynia
St James's Place 25.4.76

58 *Sagittaria Sagittafolia* Arrow-head *759*
Bulstrode 20.7.78

59 *Salvia Africana* Blue shrubby African sage *760*
Diandria Monogynia
Bulstrode 9.12.76

60 *Salvia Paniculata* *761*
Diandria Monogynia
Bulstrode 18.11.77

61 *Salvia Haemotodes* *762*
St James's Place 23.5.81
Prov: Kew

62 *Salvia Coccinea Solandri* Scarlet Sage *763*
Diandria Monogynia
Bulstrode 29.9.75

63 *Sambucus Ebulus* Dwarf elder *764*
Bulstrode 6.8.78

64 *Samolus Valerandi* Round leav'd water
    pimpernel *765*
Bulstrode 3.8.8[?]

65 *Sanguinaria Canadensis* *766*
Polyandria Monogynia
St James's Place 25.4.77
Prov: Kew

66 *Saponaria Ocymoides* Basil leav'd soapwort *767*
Bulstrode 3.[?]81

67 *Saponaria Officinalis* Soapwort *768*
Decandria Digynia
Bulstrode 15.10.76

68 *Saxifraga Granulata & Potentilla Alba* Cinquefoil
    769
Decandria Dyginia, Icosandria Polygynia
Bulstrode 5.75

69 *Saxifraga Hirculus* Marsh saxifrage *770*
Decandria Digynia
Bulstrode 9.8.76

70 *Saxifraga Hypnoides* Moss saxifrage *771*
St James's Place 22.4.79

71 *Saxifraga Oppositifolia* Purple mountain *772*
Decandria Digynia
St James's Place 13.3.76

72 *Saxifragi Nivalis* Snow saxifrage *773*
Decandria Digynia
Bulstrode 5.75

73 *Saxifraga Stellaris* Hairy kidneywort *774*
Decandria Digynia
Bulstrode 4.7.77
Prov: The Rev: Sir John Cullum

74 *Saxifraga Geranioides* *775*
Decandria Digynia
St James's Place 25.5.77

75 *Saxifraga Caespitosa* Tufted saxifrage *776*
Decandria Dyginia
St James's Place 25.5.77

76 *Saxifraga Umbrosa* London pride *777*
Decandria Digynia
Bulstrode 15.6.76

77 *Saxifraga Stolinifera* Old tyger's ear *778*
Decandria Digyn:

78 *Saxifraga Crassifolia* Siberian saxifrage *779*
St James's Place 18.4.79
Prov: Bulstrode

79 *Saxifraga Geranioides ?* *780*
Decandria Digynia
St James's Place 24.4.79
Prov: Chelsea Physic Garden

80 *Scabiosa Atropurpurea* Dark red garden scabious *781*
Tetrandria Monogynia
Bulstrode 14.10.76

81 *Scilla Autumnalis* Hyacinth *782*
Hexandria Monogynia
Bulstrode 25.9.77

82 *Scylla Bifolia* Squill *783*
Hexandria Monogynia
St James's Place 16.3.78

83 *Scilla Peruviana* Peruvian squill *784*
Hexandria Monogynia
St James's Place 28.5.79

84 *Scorzonera Picroides* Viper grass *785*
Bulstrode 13.10.78
Prov: Mr Yalden's

85 *Scrophulario Peregrina* Fig wort *786*
Didynamia Angiosp:
Bulstrode 4.11.78

86 *Scrophularia Sambucifolia* Elder leav'd figwort *787*
Didynamia Angiospermia
Bulstrode 29.6.76

87 *Scutellaria Galericulata* Skullcap *788*
Didynamia Gymnosp:
Luton 8.77

88 *Scutellaria Cretica* Skull-cap of Crete *789*
Bulstrode 8.9.81

89 *Sedum Telephium* Orpine or Live-long *790*
Bulstrode 27.8.81

90 *Sedum Sexangulare* Stonecrop *791*
Bulstrode 24.7.79

91 *Sedum Hybridum* Habitat Tataria *792*
Decandria Pentagynia

92 *Sempervivum Bituminosum Solandri 793*
Bulstrode 21.9.79
Prov: Kew

93 *Sedum Album* white stonecrop *794*
Decandria Pentagyn:
Bulstrode 24.7.77

94 *Selinum Palustre* Marsh selinum *795*
Bulstrode 4.8.75

95 *Selago Coryimbosa 796*
Didynamia Angiosperm:
Bulstrode 10.10.78

96 *Senecio Elegans* Purple groundsel *797*
Syngenes: Polyg: Sup:
Bulstrode 1774

97 *Senecio Vulgaris* Common groundsel *798*
Bill Hill 2.9.79

98 *Serapias Grandiflora* White heleborine *799*
Bulstrode 8.6.79

99 *Serapias Latifolia* Broad heleborine *800*
Bulstrode 27.7.79

100 *Sibthorpe Europaea 801*
Bulstrode 24.8.81

Volume IX

1 *Sida Occidentalis 802*
Bulstrode 27.7.79

2 *Sida Cristata 803*
Bulstrode 10.80
Prov: Kew

3 *Sida Cristata Indica ? 804*
Monodelph: Polyand:
Bulstrode 16.9.77
Prov: Kew

4 *Sigesbeckia Occidentalis 805*
Syngen: Polygam: Superfl:
Bulstrode 20.10.77

5 *Silene Acaulis 806*
Silene Acaulis Moss Campion *806**

6 *Silene Amana* Sea campion *807*
Decandria Trigynia
Bulstrode 1774

7 *Silene Armeria* Lobels's catchfly *808*
Bulstrode 1774

8 *Silene Noctiflora* Night flowering campion *809*
Decandria Trigynia
Bulstrode 16.7.77

9 *Silene Quinque Vulnera* Dwarf lychnis *810*
Bulstrode 11.6.79

10 *Sisyrinchium Bermudianum 811*
Gynandria Trigynia
Bulstrode 14.7.78

11 *Smilax Aspera* Prickly-leav'd rough bindweed *812*
Bulstrode 10.80

12 *Solanum 813*
Bulstrode 14.10.80
Prov: Kew

13 *Solanum Bonariense 814*
Pentandria Monogynia
Bulstrode 8.9.77
Prov: Kew

14 *Solanum Dulcamara* Bitter-sweet *815*
Pentandria Monogynia
Bulstrode 13.11.75

15 *Solanum Melongena* Egg Plant *816*
Pentagynia Monogynia
Bulstrode 8.10.77

16 *Solanum Pimpinellifolium 817*
Pentandria Monogynia
Bulstrode 4.10.77

17 *Solanum Pseudo Capsicum 818*
Bulstrode 2.12.78

18 *Solanum Lycopersicora* Tomatos or Wolf's Bane or Love-Apple *819*
Bulstrode 9.80

19 *Solanum Nigrum A* Dunghil Nightshade *820*
Bulstrode 3.9.80

20 *Solanum Paniculatum 821*
Bulstrode 10.11.80

21 *Capsicum Baccatum* Berry fruited Capsicum or Indian Pepper *822*
Bulstrode 23.10.80

22 *Soldanella Alpina 823*
Pentandria Monogynia
St James's Place 16.3.76

23 *Solidago Virgaurea* Golden-rod *824*
Syng: Polygam:
Bulstrode 20.11.78

24 *Sonchus Oleraceus* Sow thistle *825*
Bulstrode 26.11.79

25 *Sophora Biflora* Blunt silken leaved Sophora *826*
Decandria Monogynia
Bulstrode 22.11.76
Prov: Kew

26 *Sophora Tetraptera* A new species *827*
St James's Place 21.4.79
Prov: Chelsea Physic Garden

27 *Anthyllis Cytisoides* Broom *828*
Bulstrode 9.79
Prov: Kew

28 *Spartium Junceum* Spanish broom *829*
Bill Hill 27.8.79

29 *Sparganium Ramosum* Branched Bur-reed *830*
Bulstrode 14.8.[?]

30 *Spiraea Trifoliata* Virginian Dropwort *831*

31 *Spirae Hipericifolia* Shrubby St John's Wort Spiraea *832*
Icosandria Pentagynia
St James's Place 10.5.76

32 *Spirea Filipendula* Drop wort *833*
Bulstrode 1.7.80

33 *Spirae Ulmaria* Meadow-sweet *834*
Bulstrode 5.8.80

34 *Spirae* New species. A red meadow-sweet *835*
Bulstrode 10.7.78

35 *Statice Armeria* Thrift *836*
Bulstrode 20.11.79
Prov: Mr Lee

36 *Statice* New species. Thrift or Sea Pink *837*
Bulstrode 4.9.78

37 *Statice Limonium* Sea Thrift or Lavender *838*
Bulstrode 14.8.80

38 *Stellaria Holostea* Stich wort *839*
Decandria Trigynia
Bulstrode 5.75

39 *Stellaria Nemorum* Wood Stitchwort *840*
St James's Place 29.3.79

40 *Struthiola Virgata 841*
St James's Place 19.4.79

41 *Stratiotis Aloides* Fresh-water soldier *842*
Bulstrode 9.7.80

42 *Stewartia Malacoidendron 843*
Bulstrode 7.78
Prov: Kew

43 *Swertia Perennis 844*
Bulstrode 1780

44 *Syringa Vulgaris* Lilac White *845*
St James's Place 12.5.78
Prov: Whitehall, Dwr Dss of Portland

45 *Syringa Vulgaris* Lilac Purple *846*
Dyandria Monogynia
St James's Place 1.5.76

46 *Symphytum Officinale* Comfrey *847*
Bulstrode 1.9.81

47 *Taburnae-Montana Amsonia 848*
St James's Place 15.5.79
Prov: Kew

48 *Tagetes Erecta* African Marygold *849*
Bulstrode 10.78

49 *Tamus Communis* [Buds and Flowers] *850*
Bulstrode 10.7.77

49 *Tamus Communis* Black Briony [Berries] *850**
Bulstrode 10.76

50 *Taxus Baccata* Yew tree *851*
Diacia Monodelphia
Bulstrode 16.10.76

51 *Teucrium Marum* Mastick Teucrium *852*
Didynam: Gymnos:
Bulstrode 5.11.78

52 *Teucrium Scordium* Water Germander *853*
Bulstrode 12.8.80

53 *Teucrium Chamadrys* Common Germander *854*
Bulstrode 29.8.81

54 *Teucrium Chamaepity's* Ground Pine *855*
Bulstrode 25.8.81

55 *Thaea Viridis* Green Tea *856*
Polyandria Monogynia
Bulstrode 10.11.71

56 *Thlaspi Bursa Pastora* Shepherd's Pouch *857*
Bulstrode 17.11.79

57 *Tradescantia Virginica* A variety of Virginian
   Spiderwort *858*
Bulstrode 7.8.81

58 *Tordylium Officinale* Heartwort of Crete *859*
Pentandria Digynia
Bulstrode 6.11.78
Prov: Mr Yalden

59 *Trientalis Europaea* *860*
Heptandria Monogynia
Bulstrode 5.75

60 *Trifolium Fragiferum* Strawberry trefoil *861*
Bulstrode 22.8.80

61 *Trifolium Ochroleucum* Pale Yellow Trefoil *862*
Bulstrode 6.7.7[?]

62 *Tropaeolum Peregrinum* Exotick Nasturtium with
   Lacerated Petals *863*
Octandria Monogynia
Bulstrode 22.11.76
Prov: Kew

63 *Tropoeolum Majus* Indian nasturtium *864*
Octandria Monogynia
Bulstrode 30.9.75

64 *Tulipa Sylvestris* var: *865*
St James's Place 1778
Prov: Mr Lee

65 *Tulipa Sylvestris* Double Yellow Tulip *866*
St James's Place 1.5.80

66 *Tulsilago Alba* Colts Foot or White Butter-bur
   867
Syngenesia Poly: Super:
St James's Place 14.3.77

67 *Ulex Europaeus* Common Furz or Whins *868*
Diadelphia decandria
Bulstrode 12.11.76

68 *Vaccinium Myrtillus* Black Whortle or Bilberries
   869
Bulstrode 5.10.76

69 *Vaccinium Vitis Idea* Red whortle berries *870*
Octandria Monogynia
Bulstrode 25.9.76

70 *Vaccinium Diffusum*, Solandri *871*
St James's Place 7.7[?]

71 *Verbascum Blattaria* Moth Mullein *872*
Pentandria Monogynia
Bulstrode 12.8.76

72 *Verbascum Nigrum* Sage leav'd mullein *873*
Pentandria Monogynia
Bulstrode 27.7.76

73 *Verbascum Miconi* Mullein *874*
St James's Place 9.6.78
Prov: Dr Pitcairn

74 *Verbascum Phoeniceum* Purple mullein var: *875*
Bulstrode 26.9.78

75 *Verbena Nodiflora* White knott'd vervain *876*
Diandria Trigynian
Bulstrode 16.10.76

76 *Veronica Spicata* Spiked speedwell *877*
Bulstrode 18.7.80

77 *Veronica Triphyllos* Trifid Speedwell *878*
Bulstrode 16.6.79

78 *Veronica Virginica* Virginian Speedwell *879*
Bulstrode 25.9.78

79 *Veronica Verna* Vernal Speedwell *880*
Bulstrode 26.6.80

80 *Veronica Scutellata* *881*
Bulstrode 30.7.79

81 *Viburnum Opulus* Water elder or wild
   guelderrose *882**
Pentandria Trigynia
Bulstrode 30.9.76

81 *Viburnum Opulus* Marsh Elder *882*
Bulstrode 6.77

82 *Viburnum Timus* Laurestina *883*
Pentandria Trigynia
Bulstrode 25.11.75

83 *Vicia Lutea* Yellow vetch *884*
Bulstrode 23.8.81

84 *Vicia Cracca* Tufted vetch *885*
Diadelphia Decandria
Prov: Bulstrode

85 *Vicia Sylvatica* Wood Vetch *886*
Bulstrode 30.6.76

86 *Vinca Parviflora* New Sp. Solandri, Periwinkle
   887
Pentandria Monogynia
St James's Place 11.9.78
Prov: Chelsea Physic Garden

87 *Vinca Rosea* Periwinkle Madagascar *888*
Pentandria Monogynia
Bulstrode 9.10.77

88 *Vinca Rosea* White variety *889*
St James's Place 15.6.81
Prov: Mr Lee

89 *Viola Biflora* *890*
St James's Place 19.5.80
Prov: Chelsea Physic Garden

90 *Viola Calcarata* *891*
St James's Place 13.5.78
Prov: Hammersmith

91 *Viola Pedata* American violet *892*

92 *Viola Odorata* Common sweet violet *893*
St James's Place 9.3.79

93 *Viola Tricolor & Grandiflora* Hearts ease *894*
Syngenesia Monogynia
Bulstrode 3.11.77

94 *Viscum Album* white mistletoe *895*
Dioecia Tetrandria
Bulstrode 9.12.76

95 *Vitex Agnus Castus* Chaste-tree *896*
Bulstrode 9.80

96 *Volkameria Viermis* Smooth volkameria *897*
Bulstrode 9.80

97 *Volkameria Lanceolata*, Solandri *898*
St James's Place 3.80
From a drawing by Lady Anne Monson

98 *Xanthium Spinosum* *899*
Bulstrode 10.78

99 *Xeránthemum Fulgidum*, *Solandri* Great yellow
   Affrican *900*
Syngenesia Polygamia
Bulstrode 11.76
Prov: Kew

100 *Zinnia Multiflora* *901*
St James's Place 1.8.79
Prov: Mr Lee

Volume X

NOTE: Numbers 9, 18, 45, 75 and 79, although
   not in the British Museum, are listed in Mrs
   Delany's *Index* to the volumes of collages.

1 *Agrimonia Eupatoria* Agrimony *902*
Bulstrode 18.10.81

2 *Agrostemma Coronaria* Rose Campion *903*
Bulstrode 15.9.81

3 *Aitonia* Solandri Capensis *904*
Bulstrode 17.9.81
Prov: Kew

4 *Alcea Rosea* Yellow Holy-hock *905*
Bulstrode 11.9.82
Prov: Mr Lightfoot

5 *Amomum Zingiber* Ginger *906*
Bulstrode 1.11.81

6 *Antirrhinum Minus* Lesser Snap-Dragon *907*
Bulstrode 10.10.81

7 *Arum Maculatum* Cuckopint *908*
Bulstrode 29.8.82

8 *Asclepias Vincetoxicum* Swallow-wort *909*
Bulstrode 4.9.82

9 *Asparagus Officinalis* Asparagus
Selected by Q. Charlotte

10 *Aster Sibericus* Siberian Starwort *910*
Bulstrode 17.9.81
Prov: Kew

11 *Barleria Longifolia* Long leav'd Barleria *911*
Bulstrode 11.9.81
Prov: Mr Lee

12 *Borrago Officinalis* Borrage *911**
Bulstrode 20.8.82

13 *Budleja Capitata* Solandri, Globosa Hort:
   Kewensii *912*
St James's Place and Bulstrode 12.8.82

14 *Calendula Officinalis* Marigold *913*
Bulstrode 24.11.81

15 *Centaurea Scabiosa* Great knapweed *914*
Bulstrode 27.8.82

16 *Chinopodium Purpurascens* Solandri, Purple
Goosefoot *915*
Bulstrode 19.9.81
Prov: Kew

17 *Chrysanthemum Serotinum* Creeping Ox-Eye
Daisy *916*
Bulstrode 3.10.81
Prov: Mr Lee

18 *Collinsonia Canadensis*
Selected by Q. Charlotte

19 *Convolvulus Purpureus* var Rosea, Blush
convolvulus major. Eng. *917*
Bulstrode 8.10.81

20 *Convolvulus Tricolor* Convolvulus minor Eng.
918
Bulstrode 24.9.81

21 *Conyza Inuloides Elecampani* Fleabane *919*
Bulstrode 20.10.81

22 *Coreopsis Lanceolata* Long leav'd Tick-seed
Sunflower *920*
Bulstrode 28.9.81

23 *Coreopsis Verticillata* Larkspur-leav'd Tick-seed
Sunflower *921*
Bulstrode 26.9.81

24 *Crepis Barbata* Spanish Hawkweed *922*
Bulstrode 5.9.82

25 *Cynoglosum Linifolium* Flax-leav'd Hounds
tongue *923*
Bulstrode 2.10.82

26 *Dracocephalon Sibiricum* Siberian's Dragon's-
head *924*
Bulstrode 6.9.82

27 *Erica Concinna* Solandri, Flesh colour'd Scarlet-
flowering Heath *925*
Bulstrode 12.11.81

28 *Erigeron Acre* Blue Fleabane *926*
Bulstrode 10.10.81

29 *Eryngium Amethystinum* Amethyst Sea Holly *927*
Bulstrode 10.10.81

30 *Eupatorium Caelestinum* Heart-leav'd Hemp
Agrimony *928*
Bulstrode 26.10.81

31 *Gnaphalium Lutea-Album* Jersey Cudweed *929*
Bulstrode 20.9.82

32 *Gnaphalium Margaretaceum* American Cudweed
930
Bulstrode 18.9.82

33 *Hedypnois Hispidum* Rough Hawkweed *931*
Bulstrode 3.9.81

34 *Helianthus Giganteus* Tall Sun-flower *932*
Bulstrode 29.9.81
Prov: Mr Lee

35 *Heliotropium Indicum* Indian Turnsole *933*
Bulstrode 5.10.81
Prov: Lady Weymouth

36 *Hibiscus Sabdariffa* Cotton-leav'd Syrian mallow
934
Bulstrode 16.10.81

37 *Hieracium Pilosella* Mouse-ear Hawkweed *935*
Bulstrode 20.9.82

38 *Hedysarum Coronarium* French Honey suckle
936
Bulstrode 22.9.82

39 *Impatiens Balsamina* Balsam *937*
Bulstrode 30.8.82

40 *Lathyrus Pratensis* Yellow vetchling *938*
Bulstrode 7.9.82

41 *Lavendula Pectinata Dentata* Comb-leav'd
Lavender *939*
Bulstrode 6.10.81
Prov: Mr Lee

42 *Leonorus Cardiaca* Mother-wort *940*
Bulstrode 28.9.81

43 *Malva Parviflora* Small-flower'd Mallow *941*
Bulstrode 9.10.81

44 *Mesembryanthemum Linguiforme* var Sculpatrum
Broad tongue-leav'd Fig Marigold *942*
Bulstrode 27.10.81

45 *Mirabilis Jalapa Jalup.* Marvel of Peru
Selected by Q. Charlotte

46 *Napaea Laevis* Smooth Napaea *943*
Bulstrode 9.10.81

47 *Nicotiana Rustica* Green Tobacco *944*
Bulstrode 14.9.82

48 *Nissolia Fruticosa* Shrubby Nisolia *945*
Bulstrode 5.10.81

49 *Oenothera Biennis* Common Tree Primrose *946*
Bulstrode 25.10.81

50 *Oenothera Fruticosa* Shrubby Tree Primrose *947*
Bulstrode 7.10.82

51 *Ononis Inermis* Hud. Rest-harrow without
spines *948*
Bulstrode 27.9.82

52 *Polygonum Bistorta* Great Bistort
Selected by Q. Charlotte

53 *Pontedaria Cordata* *949*
Bulstrode 13.8.82
Prov: Kew

54 *Ranunculus Acris* Upright Crowfoot *950*
Bulstrode 31.10.81

55 *Ranunculus Repens* Creeping Crowfoot *951*
Bulstrode 29.10.81

56 *Rosa Gallica* The Red Rose *952*
Bulstrode 3.9.82

57 *Salvia Glutinosa* Gummy Clary *953*
Bulstrode 6.10.82

58 *Satureja Montana* Winter Savory *954*
Bulstrode 26.9.81

59 *Scabiosa Arvensis* Field scabious *955*
Bulstrode 1.9.82

60 *Scabiosa Succisa* Devil's Bit *956*
Bulstrode 15.9.81

61 *Sedum Hispanicum* Spanish Stonecrop *957*
Bulstrode 6.10.81

62 *Senecio Jacobea* Rag-wort *958*
Bulstrode 23.8.82

63 *Serratula Tinctoria* Saw-wort *959*
Bulstrode 28.8.82

64 *Sherardia Arvensis* Little field-madder *960*
Bulstrode 11.10.81

65 *Sideritis Syriaca* *961*

66 *Sideroxylon Lycioides* Box-thorn Iron-wood *962*
Bulstrode 18.9.81
Prov: Kew

67 *Silphium Terebinthinum* Solandri Turpentine
Bastard Corn Marigold *963*
Bulstrode 13.9.81
Prov: Mr Lee

68 *Sisyrinchium Bermudianum* *965*
Bulstrode 12.10.81

69 *Solanum Igneum* Firy-thorned Tree-Nightshade
966
Bulstrode 8.10.82
Prov: Miss Jennings

70 *Solanum Sodomaeum* Apple of Sodom *967*
Bulstrode 10.81
Prov: Kew

71 *Tamarix Gallica* Tamerisk *968*
Bulstrode 30.10.81

72 *Tormentilla Reptans* Creeping Tormentil *969*
Bulstrode 9.10.82

73 *Trifolium Pratense* Common Clover *970*
Bulstrode 26.9.82

74 *Valeriana Rubra* Red Valerian *971*
Bulstrode 19.10.81

75 *Verbascum Lychnitis* White Mullein
Selected by Q. Charlotte

76 *Veronica Multifida* Cut leav'd Speedwell *972*
Bulstrode 25.9.81

77 *Vinca Minor* Lesser Periwinkle *973*
Bulstrode 15.10.81

78 *Viola Blanda* Solandri Gentle Violet *974*
Bulstrode 21.9.82

79 *Viola Canina* Dog's Violet
Selected by Q. Charlotte

Additional Works by Mrs Delany

Since the publication of the first edition of this book the author has discovered a number of works in private collections. Galleries and museums other than the British Museum which have collections of Mrs Delany's work are also listed.

A large part of Mrs Delany's correspondence is now in the Newport Reference Library, Gwent. There are a further eighty letters in the Osborn Collection in the Beinecke Rare Books and Manuscripts Library at Yale University Library. Her Will is in the National Library of Wales, Aberystwyth.

Paper collages
Cystisus Glutinosus
Dianthus Glaucus
Epilobium Angustillium
Erica Cruenta
Hesperis Matronalis
Jasmin Officinale
Pelargonium capitatum
Pelargonium tricolor
Saxifrage Granulata
    Hazlitt, Gooden and Fox, London
Wall-flower, made at Bulstrode, October
    1781
    Royal Library, RL 27999. HM The
    Queen, Windsor Castle

Paintings and drawings
Sketchbook of ninety-two drawings by Mrs
    Delany.
    The National Gallery, Dublin
Portrait, *Master John Rogers of Dowdeswell*,
    M. Pendarves 1737.
    Colonel Richard Coxwell-Rogers
Portrait of two Dewes brothers, aged
    approximately six and seven years.
    Private collection
Portrait of Mrs Sandford (Sally Chapone).
    Private collection
Drawing, *Cornbury Park, Oxon, Cowley's house,*
    29 Oct 1746.
    Michael Hughes-Hallett
Drawing, *A view of ye improvements in ye Home*
    Quarry, the set of the Earl of Clarendon 15 Nov
    1746.
    Michael Hughes-Hallett
Drawing of Hanbury Steps, Worcestershire
    (without figures).
    Private collection
Drawings, *A view of part of Keidelston Park in*
    Derbyshire belonging to Nathaniel Curson. M.
    Delany 21st July 1746, and *Another view of*
    Keidelston Park. M. Delany 1746.
    The Kedleston Trustees
Drawings from the family album of
    William Howard, Lord Andover and his
    son the twelfth earl of Suffolk
    English Heritage

Drawing of cliffs and the sea copied from
    Revd C. Cordiner.
    British Museum
Drawing, *Rosalba Cariera after an original done*
    by herself, M. Pendarves, 1739.
    Private collection
Drawing, cartouche inscribed 'Innocence
    & Love & Peace for Evermore'.
    Private collection
    Sketchbook of drawings by Mrs
    Pendarves/Mrs Delany.
    Christie's sale of Queen Charlotte's
    effects, 1819, lot 412

Silhouettes
A hand-sewn book of silhouettes
    representing members of the royal
    family and subjects from nature.
    Royal Archives RA Add. 2/65. HM The
    Queen, Windsor Castle.

Shellwork
Shell decoration by Mrs Delany, Mrs
    Dewes and the Mordaunt sisters. The
    Bath House, Walton, Warwickshire.
    Restored by the Landmark Trust, 1992
Shell, seed and husk picture of a hermit.
    Royal Library, HM The Queen,
    Windsor Castle.

Manuscripts
Mrs M. Delany, *A British Flora after the Sexual*
    System of Linnaeus, or an English Translation
    of the Linnaean Names of all the British Plants,
    481 folios including index, dated 18
    October 1769.
    Lady Llanover wrote: 'Mrs Delany
    commenced a MSS book at Bulstrode,
    which she completed with her own
    hand. It appears to be a translation of

the first edition of Hudson's *Flora Anglica*
    published in London 1762. Includes
    appended list of the Genera in Latin.
    Notes added include one on the "Fir-
    Coned Hydnum – this was found at
    Bulstrode on fir-cones in Nov. 1769."'
    Possibly Mrs Delany copied this from
    Mr Lightfoot's MSS who wrote the *Flora*
    Scotia in English.
    Richard Hatchwell Antiquarian Books
    and Manuscripts.

Surviving Homes and Commemorative Places of
    Mrs Delany and her Family
Buckland Manor, Buckland,
    Gloucestershire, now a hotel.
    33, St James' Place, London. Mrs
    Delany's house between 1771 and 1788.
St James' Church, Piccadilly, London: a
    plaque commemorates Mrs Delany.
The churchyard at Glasnevin, Dublin, is
    the burial place of Dr Delany. The
    tombstone is inscribed: 'Patrick Delany
    D.D. formerly Senior Fellow of Trinity
    College, Dublin, late Dean of Down,
    hoping for mercy in Christ Jesus, he died
    the 6th of May 1768, in the 84th year
    of his age'.
The Delany Rooms, Mahon's Hotel,
    Irvinestone, County Fermanagh: a
    plaque commemorates Dr Delany as
    Rector of Derryvullen from 1727 to 1744.
A stone tablet on the Clock Tower,
    Chapel of Ease, Lotherstown
    (Irvinestone) declares: 'In the year of our
    Lord 1734 this church was re-built and
    the steeple new erected. Pat Delany
    D. D. Rector'.
Gloucester Cathedral: the tomb of Mrs
    Granville, Mrs Delany's mother, is on
    the south side.
Buckland Church, Buckland,
    Gloucestershire: Colonel Granville (Mrs
    Delany's father) is buried beside the
    porch.

Further Reading

Brimley-Johnson, R.   *Mrs Delany at Court and among the Wits*. Stanley Paul, London, 1925.

Brimley-Johnson, R.   'The Flora of Mrs Delany', *Connaisseur*, LXXVIII, 1927.

Burnett, D.   *Longleat: The Story of an English Country House*. Collins, London, 1978.

Curran, C. P.   *Dublin Decorative Plasterwork of the seventeenth and eighteenth centuries*. Alec Tiranti, London, 1967.

Day A. *Letters from Georgian Ireland: The Correspondence of Mary Delany*, 1731–68. The Friar's Bush Press, Belfast, 1991.

Flower, Newman   *Handel: his personality and his times*. Panther, St. Albans, 1973.

Gearey, C.   *Royal Friendships: The story of two royal friendships (Queen Anne and the Duchess of Marlborough, Queen Charlotte and Mrs Delany), as derived from histories, diaries etc*. Digby, Long and Co., London, 1898.

Granville, R.   *The History of the Granville Family*. Exeter, 1895.

Hedley, Olwen   *Queen Charlotte*. John Murray, 1975.

Llanover, A. (ed.)   *Autobiography and Correspondence of Mary Granville, Mrs Delany*, 6 vols. Richard Bentley, London, 1st series, 1861; 2nd series, 1862.

Malins, Edward and the Knight of Glyn   *Lost Demesnes, Irish Landscape Gardening 1660–1845*.   Barrie and Jenkins, London, 1976.

Paston, G.   *Mrs Delany*. Grant Richards, London, 1900.

Newton, Stella Mary   'Mrs Delany and her handiwork', *Antiques*. New York, July, 1969.

Paterson, A. P.   *The Chelsea Physic Garden*. London Parochial Charities.

Roberts, Jane   *Royal Artists: from Mary Queen of Scots to the present day*. Grafton, London, 1987.

Vulliamy, C. E.   *Aspasia: The Life and Letters of Mary Granville, Mrs Delany, 1700–1788*. Geoffrey Bles, London, 1925.

Index

Figures in italics refer to pages where there are illustrations